Pensions and Marriage
Breakdown

Other titles available from Law Society Publishing:

Pensions Act 2004 (due 2005)
Jane Marshall
1 85328 923 X

Probate Practitioner's Handbook (4th edn)
General Editor: Lesley King
1 85328 831 4

Domestic Violence, Crime and Victims Act 2004
Claire Bessant
1 85328 902 7

All books from Law Society Publishing can be ordered through good book-shops or direct from our distributors, Marston Book Services, by telephone 01235 465656 or email **law.society@marston.co.uk**. Please confirm the price before ordering.

For further information or a catalogue, please contact our editorial and marketing office by email: **publishing@lawsociety.co.uk**.

PENSIONS AND MARRIAGE BREAKDOWN

David Davidson

The Law Society

ISBN 1 85328 951 5

Crown copyright material is reproduced with the permission of the Controller of Her Majesty's Stationery Office

Published in 2005 by the Law Society
113 Chancery Lane, London WC2A 1PL

Typeset by J&L Composition, Filey, North Yorkshire
Printed by TJ International, Padstow, Cornwall

Contents

Appendices

Foreword

As is pointed out in this book, pension rights often form the second largest financial asset of those whose marriages have broken down. Wide powers in respect of pension attachment and pension sharing are now within the armoury of orders that are available to courts dealing with financial claims ancillary to such marital breakdown, with the result that off-setting against other assets and continuing periodical payments are no longer the only ways to take account of pension rights. As this book also points out, identical powers will be available in the event of the breakdown of registered civil partnerships when the Civil Partnerships Act 2004 is brought into effect. Family law judges and practitioners are enjoined to use imaginatively the available powers, including those relating to pension rights, so as to produce a bespoke outcome that is fair in the particular circumstances of each individual case. It is therefore essential for lawyers dealing with such cases (both at the stage of ascertaining the nature and value of the assets and at the stage of apportioning those assets) to have an understanding of pension rights and of the powers available in respect of such rights, even though specialist assistance will often be required before final decisions are made.

The problem for the busy family law practitioner is to find a clear and concise, but nevertheless comprehensive, source of relevant information about the seemingly impenetrable maze of primary and secondary legislation concerning pensions and about the numerous different forms of pension arrangement. That problem is solved by this book. David Davidson and his fellow authors have set out succinctly and clearly an analysis of the relevant powers that are available to the courts, followed by descriptions of the features of the many and various different types of pension arrangements, with an explanation of how the relevant powers may be deployed in respect of each such type of arrangement and with details of the implementation procedures. They have also highlighted the practical considerations and potential problems to be borne in mind, including taxation considerations (including a summary of the new simplified regime for taxation of pensions that is to come into effect in April 2006) and insolvency. Additionally, they provide summaries of the relevant reported cases.

To say that this book provides a comprehensive overview of the topic of pensions in the context of matrimonial breakdown would be something of an understatement. It provides much more than that, written as it is by experienced practitioners in the field. I know that it is a work to which I shall frequently turn for guidance and inspiration in the future when trying to understand particular pension arrangements and when trying to devise the most appropriate solution in cases where pension funds are a feature.

James Turner QC,
1 King's Bench Walk,
Temple,
London EC4Y 7DB.

Acknowledgements

This book has been a combined effort of family lawyers, insolvency lawyers, pension lawyers, tax and trust lawyers, an actuary and chartered accountants. Chapters 2 and 12 were written by Michael V. Sternberg, a barrister practising from the Chambers of Jonathan Cohen QC at 4 Paper Buildings, Temple, London EC4Y 7EX. Chapter 14 was written by James Hyne and Roger Elford of Charles Russell's insolvency and corporate recovery department with an overall editorial review by Kris Weber, Charles Russell's pensions partner and leading pensions expert. Kris has also been an invaluable source of advice on other chapters and I am grateful too for the help of his assistant, Rosamund Lee.

Jim Boyle, an actuary with SBJ Benefit Consultants has made a substantial input into Chapters 7 and 11. George Duncan, a partner in Charles Russell's private client department, has given invaluable advice on Chapters 7 and 8. Finally, I would like to thank Melvyn Segal and Simon Simpson of Arram Berlyn Gardner, chartered accountants, for assisting in editing Chapter 10 on the so-called new simplified regime for taxation of pensions.

Abbreviations

AFPS	Armed Forces Pension Scheme
AVC	additional voluntary contribution
CETV	cash equivalent transfer value
CGT	capital gains tax
EA 2002	Enterprise Act 2002
FLA 1986	Family Law Act 1986
FPR	Family Proceedings Rules 1991/1247 (as amended)
FSAVC	free standing additional voluntary contribution
FURBS	funded unapproved pension scheme
GAD	Government Actuary's Department
IA 1986	Insolvency Act 1986
ICTA 1988	Income and Corporation Taxes Act 1988
IFA	independent financial adviser
IHT	inheritance tax
LGPS	Local Government Pension Scheme
MCA 1973	Matrimonial Causes Act 1973
MFPA 1984	Matrimonial and Family Proceedings Act 1984
PA 1995	Pensions Act 1995
PP	personal pension
PRPA	person responsible for pension arrangements
PSA 1993	Pension Schemes Act 1993
RAC	retirement annuity contract
RPI	Retail Price Index
SERPS	State Earnings Related Pension Scheme
SIPP	self-invested personal pension
SSAS	small self-administered pension scheme
UURBS	unfunded unapproved pension scheme
WRPA 1999	Welfare Reform and Pensions Act 1999

Table of cases

Table of statutes

Table of statutory instruments

Introduction

This book is intended to provide practising family lawyers, actuaries, independent financial advisers and lay people with a practical guide as to the powers the courts have in relation to pension funds and the way they can exercise those powers when granting financial relief following a decree of judicial separation, divorce or nullity of marriage.

Pension funds have suffered gravely since the turn of the Millennium from the removal of ACT relief on dividends and the long, savage bear market. Many company occupational pension schemes have either been closed altogether or to new members. Life expectancy is increasing, thereby necessitating that people must provide much larger funds to give themselves a decent income in old age. There is never a day when these issues are not mentioned in the financial press. The 'grey' vote element of the electorate is growing in power. There is a real imperative for fresh legislation to overhaul and simplify the manner in which people can provide for their retirement. It is inevitable that there will have to be a continuing tax incentive to do so and it may be that there will have to be an element of compulsion if there is not to be a very serious crisis in provision for the elderly.

There is a steady increase in the number of Pension Sharing Orders being made. The legislation making them possible only came into effect in respect of petitions for divorce or nullity filed on or after 1 December 2000 so early comments that there had been a slow take-up of utilisation of this new power were wide of the mark due to a misunderstanding of the time lags in the court process. There is no proper statistical method of calculating the numbers of orders being made but anecdotal evidence obtained from family lawyers shows clearly they are on the increase. Given the economic and political climate I have described above, pension/retirement funds in whatever form they will take in years to come are going to be a significant factor in many divorce cases. The long swings of the economic cycle could well mean that by the end of this decade today's pension funds are in a far more healthy state by that date.

The Finance Act 2004 introduces a new, simplified, tax regime for all pension schemes with effect from 6 April 2006 and its main provisions are outlined in some detail in Chapter 10.

The law is stated as at 30 September 2004.

CHAPTER 1

Court orders for financial relief

In proceedings for judicial separation, divorce and nullity, the courts can make three classes of financial order on or after the pronouncement of the decree:

1.1 FINANCIAL PROVISION ORDER

This is an order for periodical payments, secured provision or lump sum. All Pension Attachment Orders fall within this category; they are a sub-species of these orders. Once a court has dismissed a spouse's right to apply for financial provision, it has also dismissed that spouse's right to apply for any form of Pension Attachment Order.

1.2 PROPERTY ADJUSTMENT ORDER

In the context of pensions the only relevant property adjustment order is a variation of settlement order varying the provisions of a pension scheme as an ante or post nuptial settlement. Since no variation of settlement order can be made in respect of a pension scheme where a petition for divorce, nullity or judicial separation has been filed on or after 1 December 2000, the use of this remedy will die out over time.

1.3 PENSION SHARING ORDER

If an order only dismisses a spouse's claim to financial provision and property adjustment orders, it leaves the claim for pension sharing alive and open.

1

1.4 DISCRETIONARY JURISDICTION

It is important to remember that the courts' jurisdiction in financial relief is discretionary and to be exercised within the guidelines set out in the Matrimonial Causes Act (MCA) 1973, s.25. There are no fixed rules. The House of Lords in *White* v. *White* [2000] 2 FLR 981 said that the courts must exercise their powers so as to achieve a fair result. What is a fair result depends so much on the circumstances of each individual case and factors such as the length of the marriage, the ages of the parties, the earning capacity and health of the parties, the ages and health of the children etc. If a pension fund or funds are a material part of the family assets in a given case, solicitors need to reflect carefully on the nature of the fund itself, the uses to which it can be put and the manner in which the courts' powers should be exercised to fit the needs and entitlements of the two spouses. Where the pension funds are substantial, they also need to consider very carefully with expert advisers such as actuaries the effect of the exercise of the courts' powers on the funds and on the benefits which either spouse may receive.

Each type of order has to be dismissed in order for there to be a clean break. This is highlighted by the fact that a lacuna in the amending legislation means that a party to a dissolved marriage can apply for a Pension Sharing Order in respect of that marriage after his/her remarriage (MCA 1973, s.28(3)).

CHAPTER 2

Development of the court's response to pension assets

2.1 HISTORICAL BACKGROUND

The fourteenth edition of *Rayden on Divorce* published in 1983, had but one solitary reference to pensions in the context of ancillary relief (see Volume 1 at p. 784). The charm of that sole paragraph, (standing solitary like the Marquis of Salisbury's foreign policy of splendid isolation) invites repetition:

> 60. *Loss of Benefit: Pension.* In case of proceedings for divorce or nullity of marriage, the Court must specifically have regard to the value to either party of the marriage of any benefit (for example a pension) which by reason of the dissolution or annulment of the marriage that party will lose the chance of acquiring. This may be particularly important in considering secured provision.

In the 1970s and 1980s in general terms, the approach of the court was based on what a party lost in pension terms by virtue of the divorce (see MCA 1973, s.25(2)(h)). By 1997 the number of paragraphs and pages devoted to pensions in what is now *Rayden and Jackson on Divorce and Family Matters*, published by LexisNexis UK, had risen enormously (see Chapter 22 of the 17th edition). It had become clear over the period 1983 to 1997 that a pension fund could easily be the single asset of second greatest value in a case.

The loss of pension rights was also considered slightly more fully, but not much, in the 1983 edition in connection with the defence to the petition on the basis of grave financial hardship under the MCA 1973, s.5(1). That defence still exists. The existence of a pension fund and hence lost benefits also arose under MCA 1973, s.10. (The author will here assume that the petitioner claimant is the wife but for no other reasons than the sake of convenience.)

MCA 1973, s.5(1) was a two-fold process: the respondent had to show 'grave financial hardship' and the court would then perform a balancing exercise as to whether it would grant a decree. Very rarely, however, did the loss of pension rights prevent the petitioner getting her decree. A husband usually found other means to compensate the wife, for lost benefits. The court would adjourn to allow him to come up with proposals, see *K* v. *K* [1997] 1 FLR 35.

Under MCA 1973, s.10, where two or five years' separation was alleged, a respondent could apply to the court for it to consider what the position would be after the divorce and to stay the decree absolute. Consideration by the court by implication included consideration of loss of pension rights where one spouse pre-deceased another so that rights might be lost. Reference must be made to MCA 1973, s.10(3) and (4) to see exactly about what the court needed to be satisfied before it would make the decree absolute: essentially it was that provision was not required or if it needed to be made it was reasonable, fair or the best that could be devised in the circumstances. Yet this requirement could be bypassed if circumstances made it desirable that the decree should be made absolute without delay and the court obtained a satisfactory undertaking from the petitioner that the petitioner would make such financial provision for the respondent as the court might approve (see MCA 1973, s.10(4)). The provision had to be detailed and specific as in *Grigson* [1974] 1 WLR 228.

Both MCA 1973, ss.5 and 10 are of course still in force and must never be overlooked.

A pension was always a resource, to which the court would have regard provided it was likely to become available in the 'foreseeable future'. But what was foreseeable? Looking further than 10 years into the future could be problematic; see *Hedges* [1991] 1 FLR 196.

2.2 OFFSETTING

How the court came to deal with taking pensions into account, before the Pensions Act 1995, s.166 and the Welfare Reform and Pensions Act 1999 both amended MCA 1973, s.25, is of more than historic interest. This is because if neither an attachment order under MCA 1973, ss.25B to 25D, nor a Pension Sharing Order is available under the amendments to the MCA 1973, then the court will be thrown back upon offsetting. This was and is most likely to happen if, say, the pension was and is an overseas one.

Offsetting was a policy of adjusting upward a lump sum payable by the party who had the pension rights to the party who did not have them in an attempt to achieve an allocation of resources within the s.25 exercise (always remembering that in the early to late 1970s, the starting point for a wife in a marriage of average length was one-third of the capital assets and one-third of joint incomes); alternatively, if there were other assets, using those assets by way of a transfer of property order to make up the loss that would take place by leaving the pension assets with the one who held them.

Offsetting carried certain drawbacks: the most important one was that there simply might not be sufficient other liquid or other assets to allow compensating transfers to take place.

When the court could not offset, it often tried to obtain undertakings from the party with the pension rights to nominate the other party for the whole or part of the death in service benefit, the dependant's pension on death and for any other pension benefit that was available (and which might otherwise fall into his estate). These undertakings often needed to last for many years which was unsatisfactory, and theoretically were also subject to variation on a further application. They also might be evaded by an unscrupulous respondent who was prepared to take his pension and himself overseas.

Undertakings could also *never* be compelled from unwilling parties, and that is still the position. The wife needed to ensure that the trustees of the fund from time to time, and certainly if they were overseas, always needed to know of the order, and regard themselves as personally bound.

The wife also had to ensure that the relevant nominations *continuously* remained in place and also to keep her Inheritance (Provision for Family and Dependants) Act 1975 claims alive in case the nominations failed.

Following the House of Lords decision in *Brooks* v. *Brooks* [1995] 2 FLR 13, where a pension scheme actually permitted an allocation of benefits from a husband to a wife there was no problem, but this was an unusual set of circumstances.

In conclusion, these days where the court has the power (unless the relevant petition was filed a considerable period of time ago) to make either a Pension Sharing or a Pension Attachment Order against a UK pension scheme, offsetting will seldom be relevant unless in the specific circumstances of the case the parties choose that one spouse will keep the pension fund and the other (normally the wife) will receive other assets in lieu.

CHAPTER 3

Pension Sharing Orders

Pension Sharing Orders will be discussed first, even though the courts had powers to make variation of settlement orders and Pension Attachment Orders some time before Parliament gave the courts power to make Pension Sharing Orders.

3.1 NATURE OF PENSION SHARING ORDERS

The court can only make a Pension Sharing Order on or after the pronouncement of a decree of divorce or nullity. It cannot make them where there is only a decree of judicial separation. The court order creates a debit to the member spouse's rights and a corresponding credit, which is a right against the person responsible for the pension arrangement, for the non-member spouse.

Pension schemes in respect of which Pension Sharing Orders can be made are the following:

- occupational pension schemes;
- personal pension schemes and retirement annuity contracts;
- Self-administered schemes;
- unapproved schemes such as FURBS/UURBS;
- the State Earnings Related Pension Scheme (SERPS);
- the additional pension element of category A retirement pension which is only payable to employees who have contributed to SERPS in any tax year;
- stakeholder pensions.

The court cannot make Pension Sharing Orders in respect of the basic State Retirement Pension Scheme or schemes or arrangements operated outside the United Kingdom.

3.2 HOW PENSION SHARING FITS INTO THE FINANCIAL RELIEF PROCEDURE

A claim for financial relief is called an application for ancillary relief. In practical terms it is commenced by Form A which is usually filed at the same time as or shortly after the petition. Where it seeks a Pension Sharing Order, which is an order under MCA 1973, s.24B, the Form A must be served on the person responsible for the pension arrangements ('PRPA') (FPR r.2.70(6)). Frequently the claimant spouse does not know what the other spouse's pension arrangements are and in that event they will have to wait until the statement of means (Form E) is served on them approximately seven weeks after the Form A is filed before formulating their pension sharing claims. However, the member spouse must within seven days of receiving a Form A together with the notice of the first appointment in the proceedings, ask the PRPA for the relevant pension information unless he/she has a valuation of his/her pension rights or benefits at a date within a year of the date fixed for the first appointment (Family Proceedings Rules (FPR) r.2.70(2)).

Within seven days of receiving the information, where it has to be requested from the PRPA, the member spouse sends a copy of it to the other party, together with the name and address of the person responsible for each pension arrangement of which he/she is a member (FPR r.2.70(3)). In practice this information usually comes with the Form E.

Most cases conclude with an agreement and a consent financial order. Where that occurs the proposed consent order must be sent to the PRPA so that the PRPA has 21 days to make an objection before the court makes the consent order (FPR r.2.61(1)(dd)).

In a contested case it is good practice to inform the PRPA of the date of the hearing. It may be that some issue will arise which will necessitate contact with the PRPA during the course of the hearing in order that all parties and the judge are clear as to the effect of any order.

However the order is made, the court must within seven days of making it send the PRPA a copy of the decree absolute, the financial order and the annex that relates to that PRPA only (FPR r.2.70(16) and (17)). In practice, the court cannot always be relied upon to do this so that the party in whose favour the order is made should serve these documents on the PRPA in any event.

The Pension Sharing Order does not take effect earlier than seven days after the end of the period of filing of notice of appeal or the

8

decree absolute, if later (MCA 1973, ss.24B(2) and 24C(1); Divorce etc. (Pensions) Regulations 2000, SI 2000/1123, reg.9). The date the order takes effect is also the *transfer day* which, pursuant to the Welfare Reform and Pensions Act (WRPA) 1999, s.29, is the day on which the member spouse's 'relevant benefits' are defined for the purposes of subsequently calculating the cash equivalent transfer value (CETV) for the purposes of implementing the actual order. This means that any payments into the member's scheme or policy after this day, or any subsequent salary rise for a member of a defined benefits occupational scheme, will be excluded from the CETV when it comes to implementation.

The PRPA has four months from the date the order takes effect or the first day on which they have received the order itself with the annex, the decree of divorce or nullity of marriage and certain information prescribed by the Pensions on Divorce etc. (Provision of Information) Regulations 2000, reg.5, to implement the order (WRPA 1999, s.34). The valuation for the purposes of the pension credit will be the figure calculated on the *valuation day*, i.e. such day within the implementation period as the person responsible for the relevant arrangement specifies by notice in writing to the transferor and transferee (WRPA 1999, s.29(7)).

The importance of these dates is something to which I will revert later.

3.3 HOW PENSION SHARING ORDERS ARE IMPLEMENTED

The WRPA 1999, Sched. 5, deals with the mode of discharging pension credits for funded schemes, unfunded public service pension schemes, other unfunded occupational pension schemes and other pension arrangements. Schedule 6 deals with the effect of State Scheme pension debit and credits.

In practical terms, Sched. 5 is the more important one and provides that, save in the case of unfunded public service schemes, the PRPA can discharge their liability for the pension credit either:

(a) by creating rights for the non-member spouse within the scheme itself (an 'internal transfer'); or

(b) by making a transfer payment to another suitable pension scheme or arrangement approved by the statute or by regulations made by the Secretary of State (an 'external transfer').

If the Pension Sharing Order is made against a member of an unfunded public service scheme, the non-member spouse will simply acquire credits in that scheme or, if that scheme is closed to new members, in another appropriate public service scheme. Such rights in public service schemes will be fully protected against inflation by indexation in the same way as those of other members of the scheme. If you act for the spouse of a member of an unfunded public service scheme, your client's potential acquisition of a pension credit in such a scheme may have particular attractions because the scheme will not go bust and the pension will be index-linked.

The legislation provides that pension debits and credits must be expressed as a percentage of the member spouse's cash equivalent transfer value. For reasons of certainty solicitors often like to draft orders so that they are expressed as a percentage that is equivalent to a particular figure. Some schemes have objected to and continue to object to orders drafted in this way but it is plainly permissible within the meaning of the legislation.

A Pension Sharing Order can be made in respect of pensions that are in payment as well as in respect of rights that are accruing. This is clear from WRPA 1999, s.27 (non-State Scheme rights) and s.47 (State Scheme rights).

3.4 WHAT CAN A TRANSFEREE SPOUSE DO WITH THEIR PENSION CREDIT?

In broad terms, if the pension is not in payment, in an occupational scheme the pension credit rights are treated in a similar manner to those of deferred members, i.e. members who have before retirement age left the employment of a company whose scheme it is; if the pension is in payment and the transferee is of an age when he/she is entitled to take an immediate pension, the credit will either be converted into a pension within the existing scheme (an internal transfer) or the relevant percentage of the cash equivalent transfer value will be paid out to another scheme which will then convert it into an annuity for the transferee (an external transfer).

It is to be borne in mind that the transferee of a pension credit from a funded occupational pension scheme is at the mercy of the PRPA as to whether or not there can be an external transfer if their ex-spouse's pension is already payable or if there is less than a year to go until the ex-spouse reaches normal benefit age (WRPA 1999, s.37, Pension Schemes Act (PSA) 1993, s.101G).

The transferee of a credit from a salary related occupational scheme, who wants an external transfer, must exercise their right to it in writing within three months of receiving from the PRPA the statement of entitlement of the amount of cash equivalent of his/her pension benefit. That transfer can be made to another pension scheme or arrangement or to purchase an insurance policy or annuity contract with an appropriate insurance company or friendly society approved under the statute (PSA 1993, s.101G as amended by WRPA 1999, s.37).

If the pension credit arises out of a retirement annuity contract, since it is not possible to create new contracts of that nature under the Income and Corporation Taxes Act (ICTA) 1988, s.618, the pension credits must be secured by a transfer either to a personal pension scheme or to an occupational pension scheme of which the transferee is already a member.

3.5 EFFECT OF A PENSION SHARING ORDER ON THE TRANSFEROR

The pension debit is a once and for all reduction of the percentage of the accrued value of the member spouse's fund. Each qualifying benefit is reduced in the same proportion, though the calculation is more complex where the member spouse is in an occupational pension scheme. Pending the introduction of the new tax regime, it is not possible to recoup those lost benefits unless the transferor was a member of a defined benefit scheme, i.e. one where his benefits depend on his years of service and is on moderate earnings, i.e. annual remuneration not exceeding one-quarter of the 'earnings cap' limited in the one year (£25,500 for 2004/2005) at the time of divorce. Members who have below moderate earnings can pay extra contributions within the annual 15 per cent limit on their employer contributions but only provided their earnings do not rise above the moderate earnings limit. Given that such people are unlikely to have income to spare, that particular allowance is superfluous in practice.

3.6 EFFECT OF INTERNAL OR EXTERNAL TRANSFER ON TRANSFEREE

This will depend on the regulations of the scheme that holds the pension credit, for example:

(a) it will not be possible to commute more than a certain percentage, usually set at 25 per cent, of the value of the fund on reaching retirement age;

(b) retirement age or the age for drawing benefits will be as set out in the Revenue Rules for the relevant scheme, i.e. 50 years of age for personal pension policies and 60 years of age, subject to certain exceptions, for members of most other schemes.

The income the transferee's spouse can draw from the pension rights will depend on his/her age. Since transfers are usually to a wife and women live longer according to actuarial tables, the annuity a wife can draw will be less than that of her ex-husband, unless the wife happens to be a certain period older than her ex-husband.

3.7 VARIATIONS

MCA 1973, s.31(2)(g) and 4(A), provide that if the decree has not been made absolute and consequently the Pension Sharing Order has not taken effect, it is an order that is capable of variation. It cannot be varied after the decree has been made absolute. The application for the variation will prevent the Pension Sharing Order taking effect before the application has been dealt with, so it must be made before the order has taken effect and before the decree absolute. If the variation application is successful, the new Pension Sharing Order again cannot take effect before decree absolute (MCA 1973, s.31(4B)).

Courts will have power to make a Pension Sharing Order on a variation of maintenance application with a view to capitalising the maintenance, i.e. achieving a clean break, relating to a maintenance order made following a divorce or nullity petition filed on or after 1 December 2000 (MCA 1973, s.31(7B)(ba)). The same restrictions apply to such orders as govern Pension Sharing Orders generally.

3.8 APPEALS

If the notice of appeal has been filed before the order takes effect, the order continues to be stayed until the disposal of the appeal.

An appeal filed after the order has already taken effect is, by definition, an appeal out of time. In broad terms, if the appellant is out of time by a short period, the delay is explicable and the merits justify a hearing of an appeal, the likelihood is that the court will allow an appeal to go ahead provided the delay does not cause prejudice. Where the delay is greater, the court will have regard to the principles applied by the case of *Barder* v. *Caluori* [1987] 2 FLR 480, HL and in *Reid* v. *Reid* [2004] 1 FLR 736 in deciding whether or not to grant leave to appeal. The court can properly exercise its jurisdiction to grant leave to appeal out of time on the ground of new events provided that:

(a) the new events relied upon invalidated the fundamental assumption upon which the order was made so that, if leave were given, the appeal would be certain or very likely to succeed;

(b) the new event has occurred within a relatively short time, probably less than a year, of the order being made;

(c) the application had been made promptly; and

(d) the grant of leave to appeal out of time did not prejudice third parties who had acquired in good faith and for valuable consideration an interest in the property which was subject to the order.

The WRPA 1999 inserts a new s.40 into the MCA 1973 which governs appeals relating to Pension Sharing Orders that have taken effect.

A possible reason for an appeal would be that the transferee spouse has died a little while after the order takes effect. Practitioners can simplify this situation if they draft a Pension Sharing Order so that there is a recital in it which foresees such an event and indicates that both parties agree that the transferor should have leave to appeal in such circumstances. The relevance of this point is that the regulations made under the legislation indicate that it is normally going to be the case that the value of the pension credit will devolve into the transferee's estate in the event of his/her death after the order has taken effect but before implementation. Alternatively, it may be kept in the pension arrangement if the scheme rules do not incorporate the provisions of the Pension Sharing (Implementation and Discharge of Liability) Regulations 2000, reg.6, enabling the PRPA to make payments to the transferee's estate. In many cases, particularly where there has been a long marriage and the transferee has fully earned his/her pension credit, it will be perfectly in order that the pension credit does pass under his/her will or intestacy.

Any application for a variation or Notice of Appeal must be served on the PRPA.

3.9 AVOIDANCE OF TRANSACTIONS INTENDED TO PREVENT OR REDUCE FINANCIAL RELIEF

The MCA 1973, s.37, has been amended so that the courts now have power on an application to restrain or set aside a disposition by one spouse to do so in relation to a disposition of rights under a pension scheme. I believe that the circumstances in which this could arise will be limited. A disgruntled husband moving overseas might have the right to transfer his pension fund to an offshore trust company beyond the reach of the English courts. Such a step could be prevented. This point applies to attachment orders as well.

Another example would be where a Pension Sharing Order is made against a spouse who is about to receive/draw benefits. He may have the opportunity to commute a percentage as a lump sum before the order takes effect, thus diminishing the CETV from which the percentage pension credit is to be carved out. If he is not prepared to give an undertaking not to receive or draw benefits in a manner that will not diminish the CETV, e.g. by exercising his commutation right, before the order takes effect, a s.37 injunction should be sought forthwith otherwise the effect of the order will be quite different from what the parties and the court intended. See Appendix O for a precedent containing an automatic undertaking within the Minutes of Order preventing this occurring.

3.10 DEFERRED PENSION SHARING ORDERS

Deferred Pension Sharing Orders were never intended to be available under the WRPA 1999. Some practitioners and courts have interpreted the legislation as permitting the courts to make deferred Pension Sharing Orders. Department of Constitutional Affairs lawyers have confirmed they can be made, though Department of Work and Pensions lawyers disagreed with them. They have been made particularly against servicemen.

They have been used where a serviceman's pension is already in payment and the non-member spouse is not yet of retirement age. By allowing the member spouse to retain full pension rights, presumably, he can afford to make maintenance payments to the ex-spouse until she reaches pensionable age. The legislation will be amended to prevent Pension Sharing Orders being deferred.

3.11   STATUTORY CHARGE

A pension credit received by a legally aided party cannot be the subject of the statutory charge.

3.12   ENFORCEMENT

The key provisions are WRPA 1999, ss.33–35 and the Pension Sharing (Implementation and Discharge of Liability) Regulations 2000, SI 2000/1053.

The basic rule is that liability for a pension credit shall be discharged before the end of the implementation period (WRPA 1999, s.33(1)).

WRPA 1999, s.33 and reg. 2 of SI 2000/1053 impose on the trustees or managers of an occupational pension scheme the duty to notify the regulatory authority within 21 days of the end of the implementation period of the fact that they have not discharged their liability for a pension credit. The Occupational Pensions Regulatory Authority can impose civil penalties under Pensions Act 1995, s.10, up to a maximum of £10,000 if the trustees or managers have failed to take all reasonable steps to ensure liability in respect of the pension credit was discharged before the end of the implementation period.

WRPA 1999, s.33(4) and reg. 3 of SI 2000/1053 set out the circumstances in which trustees or managers of an occupational pension scheme can apply to extend the implementation period.

The application must be made before the end of the implementation period. Amongst the circumstances are the fact that the regulatory authority is satisfied that the scheme is being wound up or is about to be wound up, that the transferor or transferee has not taken such steps as the trustees or managers can reasonably expect to satisfy them of any necessary matter, that necessary information has not been provided or the transferor/transferee has disputed the amount of cash equivalent.

WRPA 1999, Sched. 5 para. 10 and reg. 18 of SI 2000/1053 provide for the amount of the pension credit to be increased where payment is made after the end of the implementation period. The increase will be the shortfall between the amount it would have been if valuation day (see 3.2) had been the day on which the trustees or managers make the payment or, if greater, interest on the amount of the pension credit calculated on a daily basis over the period from valuation day to the day on which payment is made, at an annual rate of 1 per cent over base rate.

If the PRPA in question are the trustees or managers of a *personal pension scheme* they must increase the amount of the pension credit by:

(a) interest on the amount of the pension credit on a daily basis from valuation day to the day on which payment is made at the same rate as that payable on judgment debts under Judgments Act 1838, s.17; or,

(b) if greater, the amount by which the pension credit falls short of what it would have been if the valuation day had been the day on which payment was made.

3.13 OVERSEAS PENSIONS

The English courts do not have jurisdiction to make Pension Sharing Orders in respect of these as the sub-structure of statutory instruments that govern pension sharing in great detail do not apply to them. It is only if the trustees of the relevant overseas scheme are prepared to cooperate in a pension sharing arrangement that it will be possible to implement one.

In any event, practitioners should look very carefully at the rules of the relevant scheme to see if what is called a 'pension' is in any way analogous to what we understand as a pension. Some overseas pensions are quite simply another pot of capital. Hong Kong retirement funds are simply paid to the member on retirement and he/she is free to use it as he/she wishes without tax consequences. US individual retirement accounts (IRAs) are pots of money that US citizens build up during their lifetimes, but any withdrawals are taxable once they go into draw down at income tax rates.

The German pension system is particularly complex and it is possible, if the English court has made orders in respect of a German couple, for the spouses to go back to the German courts and for the German courts to make free-standing orders dealing with the sharing of pensions.

CHAPTER 4

Pension Attachment Orders

4.1 NATURE OF PENSION ATTACHMENT ORDERS

The courts were given power to make these orders when the Pensions Act 1995 inserted three new sections into the MCA 1973, namely ss.25B to 25D.

A Pensions Attachment Order can either be for periodical payments, secured provision or lump sum or sums, in each case either to take effect immediately or a deferred order, i.e. to take effect in the future.

Pension Attachment Orders can be made where the petition is for judicial separation as well as in cases of divorce or nullity.

They are directed at the trustees or managers of the pension scheme of the member spouse who fulfil the terms of the order on behalf of the member spouse.

They can be made in all proceedings commenced by a petition presented on or after 1 July 1996 where the notice of intention to proceed with the application for ancillary relief has been filed on or after 1 August 1996. The power to make them now runs concurrently with the power to make Pension Sharing Orders if the petition is for divorce or nullity and has been filed on or after 1 December 2000 and so practitioners have to consider which type of order is appropriate.

The obvious limitation of a Pension Attachment Order is that, if it is an order that the PRPA pay a certain percentage of the member spouse's pension to (usually) the wife, the pension will die with the member spouse. Contrast this with the situation where a Pension Sharing Order is made and the non-member spouse acquires an inalienable right for their lifetime. Thus, Pension Attachment Orders which are immediate, or deferred periodical payments orders or secured provision orders are likely to be infrequent in future.

4.2 LUMP SUM ORDERS

Lump sum Pension Attachment Orders have more continuing interest. They fall into two categories:

(a) an order attaching the commutation lump sum;
(b) an order attaching the lump sum payable on death before taking benefits (death in service).

An amendment brought in by the WRPA 1999 now enables the courts to require a person who can commute any part of the pension lump sum to exercise the right of commutation 'to any extent' (MCA 1973, s.25B(7)). In effect, it can order him not to exercise it at all so that any attached periodical payments order that it is making contemporaneously against the pension when it comes into payment will be effective against a larger pension. However, the power to attach a commutation lump sum does not carry with it the power to dictate when the right of commutation will be exercised, thus making the implementation of what will be an important clause in any order uncertain, in that neither spouse will know the precise date on which it will occur.

MCA 1973, s.25C provides for attachment of a lump sum payable under any pension arrangement on the member's death before drawing benefits. This is a power that is likely to continue to be used, particularly where a spouse is a member of more than one scheme and the non-member spouse will be dependent on the member spouse for periodical payments until, say, they can draw pension benefits under a Pension Sharing Order made against one or more of the member's schemes. Since a Pension Sharing Order cannot be made in respect of a scheme that is already the subject of a Pension Attachment Order, the non-member spouse could have an attachment order made against the death benefits of the member's rights under a scheme that is not the subject of any sharing order in order to tide him/her over the period from death of the member spouse and consequential loss of the periodical payments order until benefits can be drawn under the Pension Sharing Order.

MCA 1973, s.31(2B) provides that a s.25C order attaching a lump sum payable on death ceases to be variable on the death of either spouse. If the member spouse has died, the order comes into effect. If the non-member spouse dies, the member spouse will not be able to vary the order so if he/she then dies before retirement, the lump sum due under the order will be paid to the non-member spouse's estate. For that reason it is essential to draft all orders under s.25C so that they are prefixed with the words, 'Provided the [non-member spouse] does not predecease the [member spouse]' (see Solicitors Family Law Association, *Precedents for Consent Orders*, 6th edn (July 2002), precedent 59).

4.3 CHILDREN

Pension Attachment Orders cannot be made in favour of children but attachment of lump sums payable on death before drawing benefits may be ordered as a means of providing security for child maintenance/education for the non-member spouse during their minority.

4.4 STATUTORY CHARGE

The statutory charge applies to a lump sum attachment order under either s.25B or s.25C in relation to applications made on or after 3 December 2001 in so far as the lump sum exceeds £3,000.

CHAPTER 5

Interaction of Pension Sharing and Pension Attachment Orders

5.1 GENERAL

The following pension rights cannot be both attached and shared:

(a) rights in the same pension arrangement (MCA 1973, ss.24B(3), (4) and 25B(7B));

(b) rights under a pension arrangement that are the subject of a Pension Attachment Order following a previous marriage (MCA 1973, s.24B(5));

(c) pensions already subject to a Pension Attachment Order cannot be the subject of a Pension Sharing Order on a variation application (MCA 1973, s.31(7G));

(d) lump sum death benefits under schemes that are the subject of a Pension Sharing Order.

The following pension rights can be attached or shared even though the subject of a previous order or acquired through a previous order:

(a) pension rights which have already been the subject of a Pension Sharing Order made against the scheme member as a result of a previous marriage (MCA 1973, ss.24B(3), (4) and 25B(7B));

(b) pension rights acquired by one spouse as a result of a Pension Sharing Order can be attached or shared on a divorce following a subsequent remarriage (MCA 1973, ss.24B and 25B(7B));

(c) an annuity purchased, or entered into, for the purpose of discharging liability in respect of a pension credit in one marriage can be shared or attached if that spouse remarries and then divorces (MCA 1973, ss.24B, 25B(7B) and 25D(3)).

5.2 PENSION SHARING AND ATTACHMENT AFTER AN OVERSEAS DIVORCE

The WRPA 1999 amends Part III of the Matrimonial and Family Proceedings Act (MFPA) 1984 so that Pension Attachment and Pension Sharing Orders can be made in applications commenced on or after 1 December 2000 for financial relief after an overseas divorce (WRPA 1999, s.22, Sched. 2, paras 2–4).

No British pension provider is obliged to comply with an order as to pension sharing made against it by a court outside the United Kingdom. Consequently, a couple of English or Welsh extraction or who have spent a significant part of their working life in England and Wales, who move to live and work overseas and then get divorced in an overseas country, may find that they have a significant asset over which the courts of that country have no jurisdiction.

The only way in which they will be able to obtain an effective order for pension sharing will be by way of an application for financial relief after a foreign divorce under Part III of the MFPA 1984.

The foreign divorce decree or annulment decree must be one that is entitled to be recognised in England and Wales. That will not be a problem provided it was obtained by means of proceedings, that it is effective under the law of the country in which it was obtained and that at the date of commencement of those proceedings either party was habitually resident in, domiciled in, or was a national of, the country in which the divorce or annulment was obtained.

Alternatively, if it was not obtained by proceedings, it must be effective under the law of the country in which it was obtained; at the date on which it was obtained each party must have been domiciled in that country, or one was domiciled in that country and the other was domiciled in the country under whose law the divorce or annulment was recognised as valid; and neither party must have been habitually resident in the United Kingdom throughout the period of one year immediately preceding that date (Family Law Act (FLA) 1986, s.46).

If one of the parties has remarried following the foreign divorce, that party will not be entitled to make an application for financial relief under Part III of the MFPA 1984.

Under MFPA 1984, s.15 the English court has jurisdiction to entertain an application for an order for financial relief if:

(a)   either of the parties to the marriage was domiciled in England and Wales on the date of the application for leave to seek such relief or was so domiciled on the date on which the divorce or annulment obtained in the overseas country took effect in that country; or

(b)   either of the parties to the marriage was habitually resident in England and Wales throughout the period of one year ending with the date of the application for leave or was so resident throughout the period of one year ending with a date on which the divorce or annulment obtained in the overseas country took effect in that country; or

(c)   either or both of the parties to the marriage had at the date of the application for leave a beneficial interest in possession in a dwellinghouse in England and Wales which was at some time during the marriage a matrimonial home.

Where the court has jurisdiction to entertain an application for an order by reason only of (c) above, it will not have jurisdiction to make a Pension Sharing Order, so this particular ground of jurisdiction can be disregarded.

Before launching such an application, the party must obtain the leave of the court. Leave will only be granted if the court considers that there is substantial ground for the making of an application for such an order (MFPA 1984, s.13). If it is not satisfied that it would be appropriate (and that is a positive onus), the court must, as a matter of mandatory instruction, dismiss the application (MFPA 1984, s.16(1)).

It is relevant that the purpose of the MFPA 1984 is to remit hardships caused by a failure in a foreign jurisdiction to afford appropriate financial relief.

It has been held that the Act is retrospective in effect.

The factors the court has to consider in making its decision under s.16(1) as set out in s.16(2) are:

(a)   the connection which the parties to the marriage have with England and Wales;

(b)   the connection which those parties have with the country in which the marriage was dissolved or annulled;

(c)   the connection which those parties have with any other country outside England and Wales;

(d)   any financial benefit which the applicant or child of the family has received, or is likely to receive, in consequence of the divorce or annulment by virtue of any agreement or operation of the law of a country outside England and Wales;

(e)   in a case where the foreign country has already made an order requiring the other party to make any payment or transfer of any property for the benefit of the applicant or a child of the family, the financial relief given by the order and the extent to which the order has been complied with or is likely to be complied with;

(f)   any right which the applicant has or has had to apply for financial relief from the other party to the marriage under the law of the country outside England and Wales and if the applicant has omitted to exercise that right the reason for that omission;

(g)   the availability in England and Wales of any property in respect of which an order under this part of this Act in favour of the application could be made;

(h)   the extent to which any order made under this part of this Act is likely to be enforceable;

(i)   the length of time which has elapsed since the date of the divorce or annulment.

This provides a very useful checklist.

If one or both spouses has or had built up substantial pension rights here, the odds are that one or both of them has a substantial connection with this country. That connection will have to be compared and contrasted with the connection they have with the country in which they were divorced or with any other country.

Paragraph (g) is obviously highly relevant. The importance of proceeding promptly with an application under Part III is emphasised by paragraph (i).

Particularly in the case of a consent application, if a couple get divorced in, say, Australia, and one spouse has substantial pension rights in England, the other spouse has a real chance of succeeding on an application under Part III of MFPA 1984 provided the application is made promptly and the domicile or habitual residence ground can be made out. The odds are that the spouse with pension rights here could easily have a domicile of origin here and may not have given up that domicile of origin. It would be important to recite in the foreign court order that it was the parties' intention to make such an application to the English court under Part III of MFPA 1984 and, in the author's submission, it would also be advisable to have a recital that the terms of the foreign order were dependent on the obtaining of the order in England under Part III of MFPA 1984 in carrying that order into effect. It would be easier to jump the domicile hurdle because the application could be made very speedily after the foreign divorce. One suspects that in most cases the habitual residence hurdle will be harder because both parties will probably be resident in a foreign country, though there may be circumstances where one party is habitually resident in England and Wales in the 12 months preceding the pronouncement of the foreign decree or annulment.

It would be advisable that the foreign court does not make an order for pension sharing to avoid an argument that the English court has no power to make one because there is already in existence such an order, albeit that it is incapable of implementation. A recital in the foreign order of the intention to seek an order would be preferable.

The same point applies to Pension Attachment Orders, whereby the pension in payment can be attached by way of a periodical payments order, a commutation lump sum payment can be attached as a lump sum order and a payment of death benefits under a pension arrangement by way of lump sum can also be attached by way of a lump sum order. The difference is that such orders can be obtained where there is a decree of judicial separation as well as where there is a decree of divorce or nullity of marriage.

Interestingly, in the author's view, the amendment to the MFPA 1984 brought about by the WRPA 1999 is retrospective. A Pension Sharing Order in England and Wales can only be obtained under an English divorce when the petition for divorce or nullity is presented on or after 1 December 2000. The amending provisions of WRPA 1999, Sched. 12 in respect of the MFPA 1984 and the statutory instrument bringing it into force do not contain a similar provision preventing the obtaining of a Pension Sharing Order after a foreign divorce or annulment where the proceedings were commenced on or before 1 December 2000.

If there had been a contested hearing in the foreign court and, say, the spouse with the English pension rights capable of being shared in England, had utilised the foreign court's jurisdiction to prevent such an order being made, it is a moot point whether the other spouse would necessarily obtain leave to make a Part III application. The foreign court would, by dealing with the matter, have fixed the primary jurisdiction under *forum conveniens* or Brussels II principles. It seems to me that a party seeking to obtain a Pension Sharing Order after such a contested case would have a far higher hurdle to jump and would be unlikely to succeed.

5.3 REGULATIONS APPLYING TO PENSION SHARING AND ATTACHMENT

Divorce etc. (Pensions) Regulations 2000, SI 2000/1123

These Regulations replace the identically named 1996 Regulations and apply to all proceedings for divorce, judicial separation and nullity commenced on or after 1 December 2000. They apply to pension sharing and attachment, hence the inclusion of judicial separation proceedings.

Regulation 3 governs valuations and cross-refers to the Pensions on Divorce etc. (Provision of Information) Regulations 2000, SI 2000/1048, maintaining the CETV as the basis of valuation.

Regulation 4 deals with the requirements for notices when a Pension Attachment Order has to 'follow' a transfer of all of someone's rights from one scheme to another under MCA 1973, s.25D(1)(a).

Regulation 5 deals with the requirements and notices when a scheme member suffers a partial reduction of benefits, particularly where there is a transfer of some of his/her benefits. The person responsible for the original pension arrangement must give notice within 14 days of the transfer of the name and address of the person responsible for the new arrangements.

Regulation 6 deals with changes of circumstances and is particularly applicable where the payee under a Pensions Attachment Order changes address.

Regulation 9 states that a Pension Sharing Order shall not take effect earlier than seven days after the end of the period for filing a notice of appeal against the order.

Pensions on Divorce etc. (Provision of Information) Regulations 2000, SI 2000/1048

These Regulations came into force on 1 December 2000.

It is well worth reading regs 2 and 4 as they, in effect, provide a precedent for the information that needs to be obtained from the PRPA of every pension scheme. However, it is a probability that new rules will be issued in March 2005 prescribing the information to be obtained from the PRPA in a court form, so it will only be necessary to send that new form to the PRPA.

Regulation 2 deals with the requirements for provision of information imposed on a PRPA under the WRPA 1999, s.23. Different rules apply according to whether the information is required by a member, his/her spouse or a court order.

Interesting provisions are found in reg.2(3)(d) and (e) which require the scheme to indicate whether or not the transferee of a pension credit will be offered membership of the same scheme, i.e. an internal transfer, and reg.2(3)(f) which requires information to be given as to charges to be levied.

Similar time limits apply to the Secretary of State in respect of information about a spouse's shareable State Scheme rights in the Sharing of State Scheme Rights (Provision of Information and Valuation) (No. 2) Regulations 2000, SI 2000/2914.

Regulation 3 deals with the bases of valuation and, broadly, requires CETVs to be supplied.

Regulation 4 requires a person responsible for a pension arrangement to give the name and address of the arrangement to which any order should be sent and certain information within 21 days of receiving notice that the Pension Sharing Order may be made. The information to be given includes whether or not details can be requested about the member's state of health and whether the transferee can nominate someone to receive the pension credit benefit, including any lump sum which may be payable, if the transferee dies before the liability in respect of pension credit benefit has been discharged.

Regulation 5 deals with the information the PRPA may request before the implementation period of the Pension Sharing Order begins to run.

Regulation 6 deals with the situation where the transferee has died before the order has been implemented.

Regulation 7 imposes a 21-day time limit from receipt of a Pension Sharing Order on the person responsible for the pension arrangement to provide information, including notice of implementation of the order or why the order has not been implemented, e.g. because their charges have not been paid.

Regulation 8 states within 21 days of discharging liability under a Pension Sharing Order the person responsible must issue a notice of discharge of liability giving certain information.

Regulation 10 states that a person responsible for a pension arrangement must, within 21 days of receipt of a Pension Attachment Order, provide information, in particular a list of the changes of circumstances of which either party must give notice and details of unpaid charges.

Pensions on Divorce etc. (Charging) Regulations 2000, SI 2000/1049

These regulations came into force on 1 December 2000.

Regulation 2 specifies the requirements that must be met by the PRPA before they may recover charges.

Regulation 2(8) provides that no charge may be made for information/valuations, unless the information/valuation has already been provided within the previous 12 months or the request or court order for the information/valuation is made within 12 months of the member spouse reaching normal pension age or he/she has reached normal pension age.

Regulation 4 provides that where a PRPA is entitled to charge for information they can insist on payment by the member spouse before providing it.

Regulation 7 specifies that if the PRPA is entitled to charge, then on giving appropriate notice, they can insist on payment before implementing the order.

Regulation 8 provides that a payment of charges by one party to a Pension Sharing Order on behalf of the other party is recoverable as a debt.

Regulation 9 specifies methods of recovery of charges by a PRPA.

Pension Sharing (Valuation) Regulations 2000, SI 2000/1052

These regulations came into force on 1 December 2000.

These specify that rights, in respect of which a person is in receipt of a pension or income withdrawal by virtue of being a widow, widower or dependant, are not shareable. *Inter alia*, they also make provision for the calculation and verification of cash equivalents for the purpose of creating pension credits and debits.

Pension Sharing (Pension Credit Benefit) Regulations 2000, SI 2000/1054

These regulations came into force on 1 December 2000.

They are lengthy and deal with a mass of technical issues such as transfers of pension credits between schemes, the age at which the transferee can take benefits, securing pension credit benefit by insurance policies and the limited circumstances in which the transfers can be made to overseas schemes.

CHAPTER 6

Variation of settlement orders and pension schemes

6.1 GENERAL

It was only when *Brooks* v. *Brooks* [1995] 2 FLR 13 was decided by the House of Lords in 1995 that it was established that the courts had power under the MCA 1973, s.24(1)(c), in certain circumstances, to vary pension schemes as settlements.

In practice, this power only applied where:

(a) the pension scheme was set up post-marriage; and
(b) the scheme included provision for a widow.

The power did not apply to non-funded schemes (of which civil servant pension schemes are a good example) because there is no underlying fund.

Money purchase schemes, earnings related/final salary schemes, retirement annuity contracts and personal pension schemes were all potentially amenable to this jurisdiction.

6.2 PERMISSIBLE VARIATIONS

The House of Lords held that, as a general rule, no variation should affect the rights of third parties and no variation should be effected which did not have Inland Revenue approval.

The only permissible variations were therefore as follows:

(a) Where there was an occupational scheme with more than one member and a wife who was an employee, but had no pension rights of her own, the court could diminish the husband's fund to create:

    (i)   a separate fund for the wife as an employee so as to give her a retirement pension not exceeding the Inland Revenue maximum applicable to her, and/or;

    (ii)   a separate fund for the wife as a dependant to give her a guaranteed contingent dependant's pension; such a pension would require that the wife was actually a dependant, by receipt of maintenance under a periodical payments order, on the death of the husband.

        The court could not diminish the funds of any of the other members in favour of the wife.

(b)   Where there was an occupational scheme with more than one member and a wife who was not an employee, the only provision possible for the wife was to her as a dependant provided that effecting it did not diminish funds available for third parties who were also members of the scheme.

(c)   Where there was an occupational scheme where the husband was the only member and the wife was an employee, the position was as in (a) above, only simpler in that the other member's interests simply did not arise.

(d)   Where there was an occupational pension scheme where the husband was the only member and the wife was not an employee, the position was as in (b) above, only simpler.

(e)   Where there was a retirement annuity contract or personal pension scheme, the only variation permissible would be to prescribe a guaranteed contingent dependant's pension.

As previously noted, such applications cannot be made where the petition is filed on or after 1 December 2000 and they are unlikely to be made under the courts' variation jurisdiction under MCA 1973, s.31(7B) because that will not effect a clean break. It is implicit in such an order that its purpose would be for the member spouse, usually the husband, to give up a part of his pension to provide the dependant's pension for an ex-spouse, who, to satisfy revenue rules as to entitlement, will therefore have to be dependent upon him under a periodical payments order of the Court at the time of his death, i.e. there would therefore be a continuing maintenance order and no 'clean break'.

CHAPTER 7

Current pension tax regimes

7.1 GENERAL

What is described here is the pension tax regime that prevails until the new provisions in the Finance Act 2004 come into effect. The purpose underlying the provisions relating to the taxation of pensions schemes and pension benefits in the Finance Act 2004 is to unify and simplify the taxation of pensions with effect from 6 April 2006. This is intended to make pensions easier to understand and cheaper to operate. However, it is not possible to understand the proposed new unified taxation scheme without a knowledge of the different types of pension scheme and of the fiscal provisions that apply to them until 5 April 2006 (see Figure 7.1). Many of the issues and problems that arise on implementation of Pension Sharing Orders against the different types of scheme will be unchanged following the introduction of the unified taxation structure.

The new, unified taxation scheme is outlined in Chapter 10.

7.2 OCCUPATIONAL SCHEMES

Occupational pension schemes received an impetus from tax reliefs introduced in 1921 and grew hugely. Until recently, the majority provided 'defined benefits', that were almost always based on an employee's years of service with the employer company. Less common were schemes that provided benefits based on 'defined contributions', under which the employee's pension benefits were governed by the market value of the contributions made by him/her and/or on his/her behalf at the date of retirement/drawing benefits and by annuity rates. As the reader will be only too aware, many defined benefit schemes have been closed altogether or closed to new

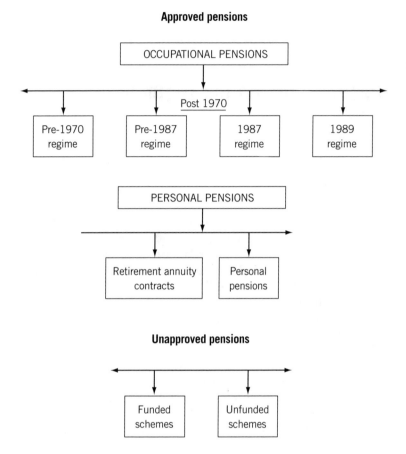

Figure 7.1   Pensions

members and defined contribution schemes now form a substantially greater proportion of occupational pension schemes.

Pre-1970 regime

Under the previous code (pre-1970), there was no limit on tax exempt and employer contributions:

- employee contributions gained tax relief up to 15 per cent of remuneration;
- in trust funds, pension benefits could be up to two-thirds of final

remuneration after 20 or more years of service, with no right to commute any of this to a tax free lump sum;
- In pension funds, benefits were the same as trust funds, with some rights to commute.

By definition these schemes were comparatively rare and practitioners will infrequently come across them.

The reference in what follows to capped and uncapped remuneration is to the earnings cap introduced in 1989 and revised each year at the time of the budget. It is £102,000 in 2004/2005.

Pre-1987 regime

The main elements were:

- pension up to two-thirds of uncapped final remuneration after 10 years' minimum service;
- tax free lump sums limited to 1.5 times uncapped final remuneration for 20 years of service;
- specific rules for early leavers, and early and late retirement;
- certain retained benefit rules, namely restrictions depending on the benefits available from pension rights from previous employments;
- employees may contribute, with tax relief, up to 15 per cent of remuneration.

1987 Regime

The main elements were:

- pension up to two-thirds of uncapped final remuneration after 20 or more years of service;
- employees may contribute, with tax relief, up to 15 per cent of remuneration;
- tax free lump sums limited by a formula of three-eightieths times final salary times years of service up to 40, with an upper limit of £150,000.

1989 Regime

The main elements were:

- employees may contribute, with tax relief, up to 15 per cent of remuneration up to the earnings cap;

- no specific limits on employer contributions with tax relief;
- total benefits, including any lump sum, limited to two-thirds of final remuneration up to the earnings cap after 20 years' service;
- the tax-free lump sum at retirement is limited to 2.25 times the initial pension, or three-eightieths of capped final remuneration for each year of service up to 40 years;
- retirement at any age from 50 to 75.

7.3 PERSONAL PENSIONS

Retirement annuity contracts

These were the first personal pension schemes and were not called such until the term 'personal pensions' came into use pursuant to the Finance Act 1988. They are pension policies that were only available to the self-employed and those in non-pensionable employment, which in general terms meant employment where the employer did not provide a pension scheme. They were initiated by the Finance Act 1956 following the Millard Tucker Report in 1956. They still exist and contributions can still be made to them by people who had such contracts prior to 1 July 1988. On 1 July 1988 it ceased to be possible to create a new retirement annuity contract (RAC):

- relief on contributions up to a percentage of uncapped earnings; the percentage depends on the age: 17.5 per cent for people under 50, rising to 27.5 per cent for people over 60;
- matured pension savings must be used to buy an annuity;
- tax free lump sums allowed according to the size of the annuity;
- it is also possible to have policies taken out before 1 July 1988 that just provide a lump sum benefit in the event of the policy holder's death before a certain date.

Personal pensions

These became available on 1 July 1988 and were introduced for a number of reasons:

- the escalating cost of SERPS, the level of which the government decided to reduce over a number of years, *inter alia*, by encouraging employees to contract out;
- to permit transfers out of occupational schemes.

The tax rules date from 1988, with some updating in 2001 when stakeholder pensions were introduced for the purpose of allowing non-earners to participate:

- relief on contributions up to the higher of £3,600 a year (see below) or a percentage of capped earnings. The percentage depends on age: 17.5 per cent for people under 36, rising to 40 per cent for people over 60;
- no limits on the size of pension benefits;
- tax-free lump sums of up to 25 per cent of matured pension savings.

The reference to £3,600 is a reference to stakeholder schemes, to which non-earners can contribute. They can pay in £2,808 a year and the government tops it up to £3,600 a year, being the basic rate tax relief. It does not matter that a third party makes contributions on behalf of a non-earner.

7.4 UNAPPROVED PENSION SCHEMES

These were rare before 1989, when employers sought ways to continue to offer generous pension benefits to highly paid employees whose pensions would otherwise have been restricted by the introduction of the earnings cap:

- employer contributions count towards employee's taxable income, with no limit, and they generally also count as a business expense against the employer's tax liability;
- employee contributions are unlimited, but do not attract tax relief (usually they do not contribute);
- no limits on benefits, which may be paid as:

  - tax-free lump sums; and/or
  - taxable income (although there is no point in taking them in this form).

These schemes are either funded (FURBS) or unfunded (UURBS). With the latter, the employer meets the costs of benefits to the employee, when they are payable, out of current income. There is no separate trust fund, merely a contractual promise; they are only as good as the employer itself, and may not vest if employee leaves before normal retirement date.

35

7.5   FURTHER TYPES OF PENSION

Private sector – large employer

These may take the form of executive category pension schemes within occupational schemes (or a separate 'directors only' scheme) – on occasions *plus* FURBS or UURBS top-up to main scheme (if the member is subject to the salary cap in respect of benefits).

Characteristics of these are:

- accrual rates are high in some post-1970 – pre-1989 schemes; it is possible to accrue a full two-thirds of final salary pension in 10 years;
- all of salary counts towards pension benefits; it is important to look carefully at the definition of final salary, particularly when it is not a capped scheme;
- multi-million pound funds are not uncommon.

Private sector – self-invested personal pension (SIPP)

In 1989 it became possible for personal pensions to be invested in different types of funds managed by life offices. SIPPs grew out of joint Inland Revenue Superannuation Board/Occupational Pensions Board Memorandum No. 101, published in 1989.

SIPPs are a form of personal pension for the financially astute, high net worth client with additional requirements because of the member's ability to control how the fund is invested. SI 2001/117, reg.3, defines 'a self-invested personal pension scheme' in broad terms as a member's arrangement(s) within a personal pension scheme in which the member has the power to direct how the funds are invested.

The member is either a trustee of his/her own SIPP fund or instructs a trustee and thereby controls the investments personally. Anyone can have a SIPP provided they are under 75, in receipt of remuneration subject to PAYE tax or self-employed with earned income subject to Sched. D tax. There is no limit to the number of SIPPs an individual may have. Retirement age is at present any time between 50 and 75, and 25 per cent of the fund can be commuted as a lump sum on retirement.

Contribution limits are the same as for other types of personal pensions.

The only benefits payable are:

- an annuity to the member;
- a lump sum payable when the annuity commences;
- an annuity payable on the member's death to the spouse or dependants;
- a lump sum payable under a term assurance contract on a member's death before 75;
- if no annuity is payable on the member's death, a lump sum not exceeding the contributions paid by the member and employer, with interest/investment growth.

A SIPP can provide some or all of these benefits.

Permissible investments are of a wide class and include:

- stocks and shares quoted on a UK stock exchange including securities traded on the unlisted securities markets such as AIM (but not OFEX), and in open-ended investment companies;
- stocks and shares traded on a recognised overseas stock exchange;
- unit trusts and investment trusts;
- policies or funds of UK insurance companies or authorised EC insurance companies;
- deposit accounts;
- second-hand endowment policies;
- foreign currency;
- futures and options traded on a recognised stock exchange including currency, equity or bonds;
- property, i.e. commercial property, farm land, forestry, public houses, hotels, motels, guest houses and nursing homes.

A SIPP can borrow to finance the purchase or development of a commercial property and a SIPP trustee may lease property to the member's business on normal commercial terms with an independent/professional assessment of the rent payable. Such property cannot be bought from nor sold to the member nor can it be acquired by the trustee(s) after the later of the member attaining the age of 65 and commencing income withdrawal from the relevant part of the fund.

SIPPs are often linked to income withdrawal/draw down for those wanting to avoid locking capital into annuities (see Chapter 8).

It is necessary to cash in the CETV created by a Pension Sharing Order against a SIPP and create a new policy.

7.6   SMALL SELF-ADMINISTERED PENSION SCHEME (SSAS)

General

These were first developed and promoted in the early 1970s as a flexible means of providing directors of small, private companies with a pension fund and simultaneously permitting the fund's money to be invested in or used by the business. They are occupational schemes of the 'money purchase' type. They operate under the Retirement Benefits Schemes (Restriction on Discretion to Approve) (Small Self-Administered Schemes) Regulations 1991, SI 1991/1614 and parallel social security regulations, which grant dispensations on investment freedom and exemptions from some aspects of the Pensions Act 1995 provided the SSAS operates under the provisions of these Regulations and provided all members are trustees of the SSAS. In 1998 there were around 40,000 in existence.

SSASs can have up to 12 members (provided that at least two are 'connected', but typically have less than this ('connected' means a relative, a partner or a co-director of another member, a trustee or employer in relation to the scheme). One trustee has to be a pensioneer trustee. A pensioneer trustee must satisfy Revenue approved criteria. He/she must not be a member of the SSAS or connected with a member, trustee or participating employer. The employers are under an obligation to fund the SSAS. They have strict reporting requirements.

Investment

After the first two years of a scheme's life, SSASs can invest up to 50 per cent of their assets in the sponsoring company and can invest in unlisted companies. They cannot invest in shares in unquoted companies carrying with them in excess of 30 per cent of the voting power or dividend rights.

SASSs can invest a substantial portion of their assets in a single property with or without the aid of a bank loan, often then leased back at a commercial rent to the sponsoring company (this counts towards the self-investment limit).

SSASs can be exempt from the need to prepare audited accounts. This can mean that getting a 'true' value for the assets is difficult.

SSASs cannot lend money to or make purchase or sale transactions with a scheme member or someone connected with a scheme member or purchase property which has, at any time in the last three years, been owned by a member or 'connected' person.

Loans to employers and other associated companies are permitted provided they are merited as a purely commercial investment decision. They count towards self-investment limits.

Asset apportionment

Assets in a SSAS are only notionally apportioned between members; it is not permitted to assign any particular asset to a single member, although the trust can be administered on the basis that members notionally 'own' specific assets for the purpose of administration.

Assets are often notionally apportioned on the basis of the maximum benefits that can be paid to a member on retirement. In cases where the members have control over the form of remuneration they can take from the sponsoring company (i.e. dividends versus direct remuneration), it may be possible to restructure remuneration in order to allow higher allocation of funds under the SSAS. Typically, the wife might be receiving a nominal salary from the sponsoring company, which might limit the benefits she can receive under the SSAS in her own right.

CHAPTER 8

Income withdrawal or drawdown

8.1 GENERAL

The idea of income withdrawal for members of personal pension schemes grew out of managed annuities that were developed by life offices in late 1993. Under these, assets were transferred from a personal pension policy after taking a commutation lump sum to a managed annuity contract backed by fixed interest investments or equities and unit-linked funds or with-profit funds. Members withdrew the cash, subject to tax, by encashing assets and left the remaining assets to grow in the contract.

A year later they were ended by the Inland Revenue due to a legal technicality.

The demand for them had grown out of the need for retiring people to try to exercise some choice over the time when they purchased annuities, to avoid doing so when annuity rates were low.

In order to plug the gap caused by the demise of managed annuities, Finance Act 1995, s.58 was introduced providing for enabling legislation in Sched. 11 to be brought into effect for income withdrawals to be made under personal pension schemes when the purchase of an annuity was deferred.

The legislation severed the link between the taking of the cash lump sum and the commencement of the annuity, which otherwise had to be simultaneous. The cash lump sum under the policy is payable on the date on which the election to defer the annuity takes effect and cannot be taken later. It should be borne in mind that most people with personal pension policies have many different policies split into segments so this election can be made on different dates for different segments of policies between the member attaining (under present rules) his/her 50th and 75th birthdays.

8.2   MEMBER'S RIGHT TO WITHDRAW

Members must withdraw income during the period of deferral. Amounts withdrawn are subject to income tax.

There is a maximum level of withdrawal equivalent to a level single-life annuity fixed by Government Actuary's Department (GAD) tables. There is a minimum level of withdrawal equal to 35 per cent of the maximum. Members can vary the level of withdrawal within these limits from year to year. Maximum and minimum levels are recalculated every three years using GAD tables and the balance of the member's remaining fund.

8.3   WHAT HAPPENS ON THE DEATH OF THE MEMBER?

If a member dies during income withdrawal, within two years of his/her death the whole of the member's fund may be paid out. The lump sum so paid is subject to an income tax charge of 35 per cent under ICTA 1988, s.648B payable by the administrator. Such a lump sum net of income tax will not normally be subject to IHT (i.e. a separate tax charge) if paid to the surviving spouse or a dependant.

If an annuity is to be purchased for a surviving spouse and/or dependant, they may choose to defer its purchase and take income withdrawal (in the case of the surviving spouse only if they are already 60). A surviving spouse or dependant cannot defer purchase beyond their 75th birthday or the deceased's 75th birthday, if earlier.

Maximum and minimum limits apply to a surviving spouse or dependant who opts for income withdrawal with rather more complex calculations.

A surviving spouse and/or dependant may instead choose to take the deceased member's fund as a cash lump sum provided the option is taken within two years of the member's death even if the survivor has taken income withdrawals in that time.

Where a surviving spouse or dependant in receipt of income withdrawal (i.e. who has not taken the fund as a lump sum) dies within two years of the member's death and no annuity has been purchased, the balance of the survivor's fund must be paid as a lump sum (subject to the 35 per cent income tax charge) to one or more of a wide range of beneficiaries in accordance with scheme rules.

CHAPTER 9

Public service pension schemes

9.1 CIVIL SERVICE PENSION SCHEMES

There are four main pension schemes:

- *Classic*

  pays a pension based on final pensionable salary multiplied by years of reckonable service and divided by 80, plus a tax-free lump sum of three times pension. Available to those who joined the scheme before 1 October 2002.

- *Premium*

  pays a pension based on final pensionable pay multiplied by years of reckonable service and divided by 60. A tax-free lump sum of up to $2\frac{1}{4}$ times pension can be taken but it reduces pension by £1 for every £12 taken as a lump sum. Available to those who joined the scheme before or after 1 October 2002.

- *Classic plus*

  combines the classic and premium schemes and is available to those who joined the scheme before 1 October 2002. Broadly, service up to 30 September 2002 counts as classic and service thereafter as premium service.

- *Partnership*

  is available to those joining after 1 October 2002 and is a stakeholder pension.

Pension benefits based on years of service are increased every year in line with RPI. There is scope in these schemes for topping up pension by buying added years of service or contributing to an AVC fund, provided total contributions are not more than 15 per cent of earnings.

9.2 POLICE AND FIREFIGHTERS' PENSION SCHEMES

The basic contribution rate for these schemes is 11 per cent of pay and *additional contributions* can be paid, subject to eligibility, to 'purchase' additional service. Previous service as a police officer or firefighter or with another pension arrangement may be transferred to add to current service as a member of either of these schemes.

Retirement is optional in both schemes at age 50 with at least 25 years' service and in the police scheme on completion of 30 years' service. It is compulsory at age 55 for ranks up to and including sergeant (police), station officer (firefighters) and at age 60 for ranks inspector and above (police), assistant divisional officer and above (firefighters).

Annual pension is assessed on service/60 times average pensionable pay (each year of service to 20 years = 1/60th and after 20 years = 2/60ths), to a maximum of 40/60ths. Commutation to convert a portion of the pension into a lump sum is possible within certain limits and according to age. Death benefits are a lump sum death in service grant plus spouse's and dependants' benefits. Both schemes have contracted-out status which means that the level of benefits paid by the scheme meets minimum requirements.

Pension 'cost of living' increases are paid with immediate effect on ill health pensions and from age 55 on age retirement pensions. Thus, the CETV of a police officer's or firefighter's pension in service or in payment between the ages of 50 and 55 will not reflect the indexation provision nor, if under 50, will it reflect the early retirement options at 50.

9.3 ARMED SERVICES PENSION SCHEME

The main features of the current Armed Forces Pensions Scheme (AFPS) are as follows.

Benefits provided

After at least 16 years' reckonable service an officer, and after at least 22 years' reckonable service, other ranks are entitled to an immediate pension and a terminal grant of a tax-free lump sum equal to three times annual rate of pension awarded on leaving service.

Reckonable service begins at 21 for officers and 18 for other ranks, so a 37-year-old officer and a 40-year-old NCO will thus qualify for an immediate pension and terminal grant lump sum.

Those who leave earlier than these periods of service, but who have completed two years' full paid service, are entitled to preserved benefits in the form of preserved pensions and terminal grants that become payable at age 60.

Dependants' benefits are paid where a member dies in service or in retirement and may be enhanced if death was attributable through service.

Calculation of benefits

With the exception of senior officers (i.e. two-star and above) and full time reservists, pension benefits are not calculated directly on the pay of the individual member but are based on representative rates of pay for each rank – these are published each year.

For regular officers other than senior officers, the formula for calculating immediate service pensions is 28.5 per cent of representative pay after 16 years' reckonable service, rising evenly to 48.5 per cent of representative pay after 34 years' reckonable service.

For regular other ranks, the formula is 31.833 per cent after 22 years' reckonable service, rising evenly to 48.5 per cent of representative pay after 37 years' reckonable service.

Thus, a regular officer or other rank, who joined at 21 or 18 respectively, is entitled to a pension of 48.5 per cent representative pay on retirement at age 55 and a tax-free terminal grant of three times the annual rate of pension.

The key point is that where a member leaves service with an immediate pension before age 55, the pension award is fixed in amount until he/she reaches that age. At 55 it is increased as per all increases in the RPI since the member left service and continues to increase in line with RPI thereafter. Thus, the CETV of a service person who has retired before the age of 55 will not reflect this potential increase.

Senior officers receive a maximum of 50 per cent of pensionable salary, if they retired after 1 June 1998, having completed 34 years' reckonable service.

There are special provisions for medical and dental officers and those who serve on full time reserve service.

Preserved pensions

For regular officers, they are normally calculated at 3 per cent of the full career pension for each year of reckonable service, for regular other ranks they are calculated at 2.75 per cent. A preserved terminal grant equal to three times the rate of pension is also paid at age 50.

Death benefits

A pension of normally one-half of the member's pension if he/she dies in retirement, or one-half of the pension he/she would have received on non-attributable invaliding if he/she dies in service, is paid to eligible widows or widowers – also for dependent children, up to one-half member's entitlement but no one child can receive more than one-quarter of the pension. Children's pensions normally stop at 17 years, although they may continue during further education or training.

A tax-free lump sum is payable on death in service of approximately one year's salary or terminal grant payable on non-attributable invaliding, whichever is greater.

If a member dies in retirement before preserved benefits become payable, the widow or widower may receive a gratuity equal to the preserved terminal grant. Importantly, members have no power to nominate who shall receive death benefits.

Divorce extinguishes entitlement to widow's or widower's death benefits.

Attachment orders and ex-service personnel

The lump sum terminal grant payable in the future as well as the periodic pension can be attached.

Particular points on pension sharing and service personnel's pensions

The transferee of a pension credit cannot transfer such rights out of the AFPS, in common with the position under all other unfunded public service schemes.

If a member is purchasing added years, the added years he/she has bought to the date the order takes effect will be included in the CETV calculation.

Pension credit benefits are not paid to the former spouse until age 60.

If the original scheme member has not yet received a terminal grant, the pension credit member will receive both the appropriate percentage pension and a lump sum of three times the annual rate of that pension; if, on the other hand, the terminal grant has already been paid to the scheme member, the pension credit member will not receive a lump sum as well as a percentage of the pension.

The pension credit member's pension, *when paid*, will be revalued in line with the increases in the RPI.

Additional voluntary contributions (AVCs) may not be made to enhance pension credit benefits.

Where the member's pension is already in payment, he/she will receive a reduced pension from the date the Pension Sharing Order comes into effect. The reduced pension will be uprated in line with the RPI in the normal way. There is likely to be an overpayment between transfer day and the date of implementation, which will be recovered subsequently from the scheme member.

9.4 TEACHERS' PENSION SCHEME

Members of the scheme are contracted out of SERPs. They pay 6 per cent of their salary. Their employer pays a further 13.5 per cent with effect from 1 April 2003. These rates of payment are reviewed by the government actuary at regular intervals. Despite this, the scheme is only funded by a small reserve fund to cover cashflow, i.e. the contributions are only used to meet current outgoings.

Retirement age is 60. Pension is based on 1/80th of final salary times each year of reckonable service. Final average salary = highest amount of full time salary for any successive 365 days of pensionable employment during the last three years of such employment (subject to earnings cap if the member joined the scheme on or after 1 June 1989). In addition, a member is entitled to a lump sum of salary times 3/80.

Members in good health can allocate part of pension to provide a better widow's, widower's or nominated dependant's pension.

In the event of death in service or within a year of leaving pensionable employment because of ill health and whilst not receiving ill health pension, a lump sum of two times final average salary is payable.

Members can buy in past added years at full cost which would otherwise not count for benefits. They can pay AVCs through the

Prudential and pay free standing additional voluntary contributions (FSAVCs). AVCs and FSAVCs may be subject to pension sharing, but as they are paid into separate funds they are excluded from teachers' pensions' CETV calculations. Ideally, a separate Pension Sharing Order should apply to AVCs/FSAVCs. If they are included on the same one as the teachers' pensions' scheme benefits, it is important to note that the order must clearly specify how each scheme's benefits are to be split. A separate copy of the order must be sent to the AVC/FSAVC scheme for their implementation. The teachers' pension scheme will make an additional charge if required to liaise with an AVC scheme.

Under the rules of the teachers' pension scheme, if the former spouse dies after the Pension Sharing Order has taken effect but before it has been implemented, pension sharing will proceed.

Pensions are index-linked in payment.

9.5 LOCAL GOVERNMENT PENSION SCHEME

The main features of the Local Government Pension Scheme (LGPS) are:

- a pension based on final pay (pay in the last year before retirement or one of the previous two years if pay was higher then) multiplied by total membership (years of service including years purchased or transferred from a previous scheme) and divided by 80;
- a lump sum of 3/80ths of final pay for every year of total membership;
- normal retirement date is 65 but voluntary retirement can be taken at 60 with reduced benefits;
- pensions are indexed in line with RPI from age 55;
- widow(er)'s and eligible children's pensions;
- a death in service lump sum of two times final pay;
- contributions of 6 per cent of pay;
- the ability to increase pension by paying additional LGPS contributions to purchase additional years of service;
- making AVCs to a separate fund.

On a pension debit being made pursuant to a Pension Sharing Order, the amount of the pension debit is increased in line with the rise in the RPI between the date of implementation of the order and the date the member spouse's benefits become payable.

A pension credit member will either become a member of the scheme (i.e. an internal transfer) to take benefits from, normally, age 65 with a pension that will be indexed once in payment, or can take an external transfer to another qualifying scheme.

9.6 NHS PENSION SCHEME

This provides on retirement:

- a pension based on 1/80th of pay at retirement for each year of scheme membership;
- a tax-free lump sum equal to three times pension;
- widow(er)'s/ dependant's pensions.

On death in service it provides:

- a lump sum of two years' pay;
- widow(er)'s/dependant's pensions.

The contribution rate for most members is 6 per cent of pay and members can pay AVCs.
As in the LGPS:

- the amount of the pension debit is increased in line with the rise in the RPI between the date of implementation and the date the member spouse receives their benefits;
- the pension credit member holds benefits in the NHS Pension Scheme in their own right (an internal transfer);
- if the order is made before the member spouse's retirement the pension credit member receives an annual indexed pension plus a lump sum equal to three times pension payable at age 60;
- if the Pension Sharing Order is made after the member's retirement, only an annual indexed pension is payable.

9.7 REVIEW OF PUBLIC SERVICE PENSION SCHEMES

It should be noted that the government is reviewing the terms of public service pension schemes, particularly with a view to phasing in later retirement ages under some schemes.

CHAPTER 10

New simplified regime for taxation of pensions

The Finance Act (FA) 2004 has introduced a new simplified taxation regime for pensions, which will come into effect on 6 April 2006 (to be known as 'A Day'). It replaces eight tax regimes with a single regime.

10.1 LIFETIME ALLOWANCE

There will be a single lifetime allowance on the amount of pension savings that can benefit from tax relief. The value of the lifetime allowance will be as follows:

Fiscal Year

2006/07	£1.5m	
2007/08	£1.6m	) These increases in allowance have been
2008/09	£1.65m	) announced but are not in the FA
2009/10	£1.75m	) 2004 itself.
2010/11	£1.8m	)

Thereafter, the lifetime allowance will be reviewed quinquennially.

Valuing a defined contribution fund by way of comparison to the lifetime allowance will be simple because the fund has a quoted market value. The valuation of a defined benefit pension scheme is more complex. Such schemes will have a single valuation factor of 20:1, i.e. £20 of capital for every £1 of annuity. An individual whose pension rights have crystallised on 5 April 2006, broadly someone who is entitled to a pension at that date, will have a valuation factor of 25:1, i.e. £25 of capital for each £1 of annuity, reflecting the fact that such individuals will generally have taken tax-free lump sums.

Highly paid executives, professional people who have earned well over years and made substantial contributions to pension schemes and top ranking public servants, including High Court judges, may well find that the value of their pension funds as at 6 April 2006 exceeds the lifetime allowance. For people in such situations it is important to bear in mind the transitional provisions which are dealt with at 10.8 below.

10.2 ANNUAL ALLOWANCE

This will be initially set at £215,000 and increases steadily each year between 2006 and 2010 as follows:

Fiscal Year

2006/07	£215,000		
2007/08	£225,000	)	These increases in allowance have been
2008/09	£235,000	)	announced but are not in the FA
2009/10	£245,000	)	2004 itself.
2010/11	£255,000	)	

This allowance will be for contributions to defined contribution schemes or increases in accrued benefits in defined benefit schemes.

After 2010 the level of the annual allowance will be reviewed quinquennially.

This is a very high annual allowance against which tax relief at the highest rate can be claimed, particularly for those paying into personal pension schemes. It is self evident that not many such annual payments can be made without an individual achieving a fund in excess of the lifetime allowance with the consequence that they will suffer a tax penalty in due course when drawing on that allowance. However, the new simplified annual allowance is plainly of benefit to those whose earnings fluctuate wildly from year to year, enabling them to have a contribution holiday in lean years and achieve substantial tax relief in fat years.

A contribution in a defined contribution scheme or an increase in accrued benefits in a defined benefits scheme (which will be confined to the very best executive schemes) in excess of the annual allowance will suffer a taxation charge of 40 per cent. In other words, an individual in a defined benefit scheme who receives an increase in their accrued benefits in excess of £215,000 in a tax year will be taxed at

40 per cent on that excess. Plainly, a person paying into a personal pension scheme (a defined contribution scheme) is unlikely to be foolish enough to pay more than the annual allowance in any one year. Tax relief for someone paying into a personal pension scheme will, of course, be limited by the amount of their relevant earnings in any fiscal year so *only* those earning more than the limit of the annual allowance can obtain full tax relief on paying the maximum annual allowance.

Employers will continue to be able to claim a deduction in computing profits chargeable to UK tax for employer contributions paid to a registered pension scheme.

For those in defined benefit schemes, the increase in their accrued benefits in any year will be measured for purposes of determining whether it has exceeded the annual allowance by a valuation factor of 10:1, i.e. £10 of capital for every £1 increase in prospective annual pension. Thus, an increase in excess of £21,500 in their prospective annual pension in the fiscal year 2006–07 will trigger the excess tax charge.

10.3   AGE FOR DRAWING BENEFITS

As of 6 April 2006 the minimum pension age will be 50, save for those suffering ill health. County cricketers and professional footballers of the future will not be able to draw pensions at the end of their playing careers, as they can do at present. The minimum pension age will rise to 55 by 2010, though those with certain existing contractual rights to draw a pension earlier may have that right protected. There will also be a special protection for people such as county cricketers and professional footballers who are members of approved schemes in existence before April 2006 with earlier than normal retirement ages.

It will no longer be necessary for a member to leave employment in order to access an employer's occupational pension. Members of some occupational pension schemes may, where the scheme rules allow, continue working for the same employer whilst drawing retirement benefits.

10.4   DEATH BENEFITS

These will be in the form of either a lump sum, a pension to one or more dependants or a combination of lump sum and pension, and what the benefits will be will depend, as now, on whether the benefit is in payment at the time of the member's death and the age of the member at death.

10.5   AGE FOR SECURING PENSIONS

It will remain a requirement that pensions are secured by the age of 75. However, it will be possible to take pension income after age 75 through Alternatively Secured Income. The minimum limit under Alternatively Secured Income will be £1, with a maximum of 70 per cent of the value of the most competitive flat rate, single life annuity available on the open market for a 75-year-old regardless of how old the member is. On death the fund has to be paid out to any survivor as income or go back to the Scheme, or be paid to a chosen charity.

10.6   TAX CHARGE ON EXCESS OVER LIFETIME ALLOWANCE

This will be 25 per cent. It will be possible to draw such funds in the form of a lump sum but that will be self-defeating as the charge will then be at the rate of 55 per cent.

10.7   MAXIMUM PERMISSIBLE TAX-FREE LUMP SUM

This will be quite simply 25 per cent of the value of the pension rights up to a limit of 25 per cent of the lifetime allowance, where a fund is worth as much as the maximum lifetime allowance.

10.8   TRANSITIONAL PROVISIONS

Primary protection

This will be given to the value of pre-April 2006 pension rights and benefits which at 6 April 2006 are already in excess of £1.5m.

Thus, an individual who has pension rights valued in excess of £1.5m at 6 April 2006 can register that value. Registered values will be expressed as a percentage of the lifetime allowance, for example, an individual who has a fund at £2.25m on 6 April 2006 will register a percentage of 150 per cent. That value will be automatically indexed in parallel with the indexation of the lifetime allowance. Thus, when the pension vests or, in the words of the FA 2004, has 'crystallised', the individual can take benefits, based on this example, up to 150 per cent of the value of the statutory lifetime allowance in that year without incurring any tax liability under the recovery charge of 25 per cent. To take a more extreme example, a high-flying public company executive whose pension rights are valued at £4.5m at 6 April 2006 will be able to take benefits up to 300 per cent of the value of the statutory lifetime allowance in the year he/she does so, without incurring the tax recovery charge. That protection will extend to their tax-free lump sum entitlement. To follow the above examples, the individual with a fund worth £2.25m at 6 April 2006 with a tax-free lump sum entitlement of, say, £562,500, will be able to take that sum increased to the same extent as the increase in the lifetime allowance. The high-flying executive with a fund with benefits worth £4.5m on 6 April 2006 with a lump sum entitlement of, say, £1,125,000, will be able to take that sum increased to the same extent as the increase in the lifetime allowance, on the date when he/she draws his/her benefits after 6 April 2006.

Enhanced protection

This will be available to individuals who cease active membership of or contribution to approved pension schemes by 6 April 2006. Provided that they do not resume active membership or contribution to any scheme, all benefits coming into payment after 5 April 2006 will normally be exempt from the lifetime allowance charge. Enhanced protection will obviously be utilised by those of younger years who already have built up funds below the amount of the lifetime allowance but which it is clearly foreseeable will grow to a figure in excess of that allowance by the time they retire and draw benefits. Some such individuals, particularly those with retirement annuity contracts dating back to pre-1988, will be entitled to a tax-free lump sum in excess of 25 per cent of the value of their pension benefit. At vesting they will be able to take the tax-free lump sum to which they are entitled on 6 April 2006, increased to the same extent as the increase in the lifetime allowance to the date of vesting. So, in the example of an individual with a fund worth £1.2m at 6 April 2006 with a lump sum entitlement of £350,000, who does not take benefits until some years after 6 April 2006, say on 6 April 2010, by which time his pension fund has grown to £2,000,000: the amount of tax-free lump sum he will be able to draw will have increased by 20 per cent (i.e. the ratio of increase in the lifetime allowance (£300,000) to the lifetime allowance at 6 April 2006 of £1.5m).

An individual who has registered enhanced protection who then resumes active membership of a pension scheme whether with an employer or by paying contributions to a personal pension at any time before he reaches the age of 75, will have protection from the recovery charge determined by the 6 April 2006 pension value. For those whose pension value did not exceed £1.5m at 6 April 2006, their personal lifetime allowance will be 100 per cent of the lifetime allowance. For those who registered for *primary protection*, because their registered pension value exceeded £1.5m, their personal lifetime allowance will revert to the percentage of the lifetime allowance which corresponded to the value of their pre-6 April 2006 fund.

Time limit for registering for primary or enhanced protection

Those seeking protection under the transitional provisions must register their pre-6 April 2006 rights and provide all necessary valuation information by 6 April 2009.

When the lifetime allowance will apply

The lifetime allowance will apply on a 'benefit crystallisation event':

- when a benefit comes into payment from a fund or a part of a fund, e.g. taking a pension at retirement or on commencing income drawdown, or the designation of money purchase assets as available for the payment of an unsecured pension;
- on there being an increase to a pension in payment above that assumed by the factor used to value the benefit against the lifetime allowance;
- when the individual member achieves the age of 75 in a defined benefit scheme without his/her pension having come into payment;
- when the individual member becomes entitled to a lump sum;
- on a person being paid a lump sum death benefit in respect of the individual member;

- on the transfer of sums or assets under a UK scheme to a recognised overseas pension scheme in connection with the individual's membership of that scheme.

Where, as will commonly be the case with self-employed people, pension income is being drawn from a pension fund under an income withdrawal arrangement/income drawdown arrangement, the annual level of pension in payment for calculating the lifetime allowance will be deemed to be the maximum permitted annual income determined at the most recent valuation review of the fund.

10.9   PENSION SHARING UNDER THE NEW SIMPLIFIED TAX REGIME

Where Pension Sharing Orders take effect after 6 April 2006, the pension credit transferred under a Pension Sharing Order will count against the transferee's lifetime allowance but the pension debit will not be counted towards the transferor's lifetime allowance. Thus, the transferor will be able to make up, provided his/her income is sufficiently high, the diminution of his/her fund by paying substantial contributions within the annual allowance in future years so as to bring it up to the lifetime allowance. Neither pension debits nor credits will count towards the annual allowance.

Where a Pension Sharing Order is made against a pension in payment after 6 April 2006, the transferee of the credit will get an uplift in their lifetime allowance equivalent to the CETV they acquire because it will previously have been tested against the transferor's lifetime allowance.

Pension credits will not count towards the transferee's annual allowance.

Transitional rules will apply for Pension Sharing Orders in existence at 6 April 2006. In calculating the value of the transferor's pension rights prior to 6 April 2006, the value of the pension debit allocated to his/her spouse will be deducted.

Any individual can register pension credit rights in the same way as other members of pension schemes, particularly where those rights are so substantial that they already exceed the lifetime allowance at 6 April 2006 so that they require primary protection or it is foreseeable that their rights will exceed it in the future when pension benefits are drawn, in which case they will register for enhanced protection. Indeed, there is provision for someone seeking enhanced protection for a pension credit to be able to index the pension credit as per the increase in RPI from the date the pension credit took effect to April 2006. Thus, if you are dealing with a case involving very substantial pension rights prior to 6 April 2006, there will be advantages to a prospective transferee in obtaining and implementing an order before 'A Day' so the client can avail him/herself of enhanced or primary protection.

When acting in a case where one spouse has sufficient pension rights to qualify for either primary or enhanced protection and those rights are in a defined benefit scheme or are being taken by income withdrawal, it is important to remember that their valuation for the purposes of such protection are based on the multiples mentioned in 10.1 above and not on the CETV.

For example, a transferor husband will have (pre-A Day) or has (post-A day) primary protection. The question of whether post the Pension Sharing Order he can resume payments to a pension fund will depend on the valuation of his pension rights post pension debit after applying the relevant multiple. Solicitors must be alert to this issue but cannot advise on it under the FSMA. The client must be referred to an actuary or a G60 qualified IFA.

10.10   CHANGES TO PERMISSIBLE INVESTMENTS IN PENSION SCHEMES

Under the new regime, pension schemes will be able to invest in all types of investments, including residential property. There will be a limit on holding shares in the sponsoring employer's company of 5 per cent of the fund value and on loans to employers. However, any investment entered into before 6 April 2006 will not be affected by the new rules but where after that date, there is a change in the terms of a loan made by a scheme before 6 April 2006, the whole loan will be subject to the new rules.

Lest people think that buying residential property for occupation will be a wonderful way of building up a pension scheme, there will be a tax charge on the member for any non-commercial use of an asset by a member or an associate of a member as it will be a pension benefit in kind charge.

10.11 PARTNERSHIP ANNUITIES

Partnership annuities are not akin to approved pension arrangements and will not be the subject of the lifetime allowance or the recovery charge. Nor will the capital used to secure them count towards the annual allowance.

10.12 INHERITANCE TAX AND DEATH BENEFITS

The question of whether or not a death benefit paid by a pension scheme will be subject to IHT will depend, as now, on whether or not it is paid to the deceased's estate as of right, in which case it will be liable to it, or on a discretionary basis by the PRPA, in which event death benefits will not normally be liable to IHT.

10.13 REGISTERED AND UNREGISTERED SCHEMES

Registered schemes will quite simply operate under the tax regime described above. Non-registered schemes can continue but without any tax advantages. They will suffer the treatment of any other arrangement to provide benefits for employees. The amounts in them, i.e. in FURBS, will not be tested against the lifetime allowance and the lifetime allowance charge will not apply to them.

FURBS and UURBS cannot be treated as registered pension schemes under the new regime unless they choose to register and meet the conditions required.

Employer payments to non-registered pension schemes will not be taxable or liable to NICs as they are made, nor will the employer receive any deduction for its contributions until benefits start to be paid to, and taxed on, the employee; the investment income and capital gains received and liable to UK tax by non-registered pension schemes set up by way of a trust will be liable to the rate of tax applicable to trusts.

Non-registered schemes which are discretionary trusts will be subject to IHT charging rules.

There will be no NIC charge on benefits paid out that are within the limit of benefits that can be paid out of a registered scheme.

Benefits paid out, whether by lump sum or pension, from an unregistered FURBS or UURBS will be fully subject to tax at the member's marginal rate.

10.14   TRANSITIONAL PROTECTION OF NON-REGISTERED SCHEMES

Where, before 6 April 2006, an employee has been taxed on employer contributions when made to a FURBS, contributions can continue to be made and then an adjustment will be made to the tax-free element of any lump sum benefit finally paid out.

Amounts in the FURBS at 6 April 2006 will continue to retain their IHT treatment, i.e. not be liable to IHT, but additional contributions made after that date will require an apportionment of the fund payable on death for IHT purposes.

Where the employee has not been taxed on contributions as they were made to a FURBS, there will be no transitional provisions for the fund in existence before 6 April 2006.

Any UURBS in place on 5 April 2006 may be consolidated and rolled into a registered scheme within three months of 6 April 2006. The increase in the value of benefits in the registered scheme caused by the incorporation of UURBS will not count towards the annual allowance but will be tested against the lifetime allowance on vesting.

An UURBS consolidated and rolled into a registered scheme at any time after three months after 6 April 2006 will count towards both the annual allowance and the lifetime allowance.

An approved scheme will have the choice of opting out of the new regime at 6 April 2006 but, if it does so, the new regime will impose a 40 per cent tax charge on fund assets immediately before opt out.

Funds drawn from an approved scheme that takes this step after 6 April 2006 will be liable to tax and NIC with no entitlement to a tax-free lump sum.

CHAPTER 11

Implementation

11.1 GENERAL

Note the importance of the valuation day, referred to above (see 3.2). Welfare Reform and Pensions Act 1999, s.29 is the key governing section. See 3.2 for the date the pension debit and credit take effect. That is also the date on which the relevant benefits of the member spouse are defined. The non-member spouse will receive the specified percentage of the CETV of the relevant benefits on the valuation day, which is the day within the implementation period the PRPA specifies by notice in writing to the transferor and transferee.

11.2 FINAL SALARY OCCUPATIONAL SCHEME

A change in the member spouse's salary between the date the order is made and the date it takes effect will affect the CETV of the relevant benefits considerably.

Should the non-member spouse, if they have the option, take an internal or external transfer? This is a matter for specialist, actuarial advice, but it may well be the case that with current market annuity rates the transferee will do better to take an internal transfer, as that will provide a larger annuity than the same fund applied to an external scheme.

If the PRPA refuses an internal transfer, it may well be worth trying to put pressure on the trustees by pointing out to them that accepting the transferee spouse as a member will not involve any cost to other members.

If a transferee is considering an internal transfer, there is a need to consider the security of benefits and whether there is any possibility of the pension scheme terminating and only being able to finance a proportion of its liabilities.

11.3   FURBS AND UURBS

To all intents and purposes, a FURBS can be treated in a similar manner to money purchase pension schemes. Three particular issues need to be noted:

- transfers can only be to another FURBS, which may be expensive to establish and administer;
- the investment build-up in a FURBS is subject to income tax and CGT;
- the proceeds of a FURBS can be taken as tax-free cash at retirement.

This means that FURBS are not directly comparable with other forms of pension, and in some cases may be more attractive to the pension credit member, particularly where the pension credit member is able to realise an immediate tax-free cash sum.

The nature of UURBS can be a problem as there are no assets to share other than an unfunded promise made by an employer. This lack of security can make it difficult to put a value on them. Although they are subject to the normal transfer value regulations, in practice, transfers are rarely paid as the trustees do not hold any assets they can transfer.

11.4   RACs, PPs AND SIPPs

Retirement annuity contracts (RACs), personal pensions (PPs) and self-invested personal pensions (SIPPs) operate on a similar principle, but there are a few things to look out for, particularly where the pension portfolio consists of a number of policies, often labelled 'personal pensions'. It is important to identify which are PPs or SIPPs and which are RACs. Particular issues to beware of are as follows.

Internal transfer is not available under a RAC; the ex-spouse is forced to take a CETV to another pension arrangement.

The basis for calculating tax-free cash is not the same under PPs/SIPPs and RACs, so there may be advantage to one or other party in having a greater share of a policy of one type or other.

Guaranteed annuity rates might be available to the policy holder (more likely under a RAC than under a PP or a SIPP), but the guarantee usually only applies if the fund is applied to buy an annuity on a specified maturity date, in a specified form, and for the policy holder. Generally, there is no allowance in the CETV for the value of the guarantee, so it is possible that the policy holder can obtain better value if he/she retains as much of this policy in his/her own name as possible. Any pension share in favour of the ex-spouse will lose the benefit of the guaranteed annuity rates. If the RAC with a guarantee is one of a series of RACs which do not have guarantees, agreement to apportion non-guaranteed RACs at a higher level than the guaranteed RAC could be in the policy holder's interest. There is no requirement to share all policies in the same proportion, but care is required as the Pension Sharing Order might have to refer to each policy and the appropriate proportionate pension share for that policy.

If the policy holder is a high earner with earnings significantly greater than the earnings cap, he/she may have scope to make higher contributions to the RAC than to a personal pension. Keeping the RAC open in the name of the policy holder can therefore be of benefit.

Investment risk is inherent in any investment vehicle. There can be a significant time delay between the date policies are valued and the date the order is issued. There can be a four-month delay before the order is implemented.

11.5   INCOME WITHDRAWAL OR DRAWDOWN AND PERSONAL PENSION POLICIES

See also Chapter 8. In recent years, rightly or wrongly, individuals with substantial pension funds often have been advised not to buy an annuity for retirement, but instead to draw income from their fund within limits using Government Actuary's Department (GAD) tables.

This does not in itself present any special difficulties, since the CETV is easy to obtain, and the procedure for obtaining and implementing a Pension Sharing Order is not changed. A holder of a RAC has to convert it into a Personal Pension policy in order to effect drawdown. There are a few practical issues to look out for.

It is only necessary to recalculate the income drawdown limit every three years. If the member taking income drawdown had the level of income he/she could draw last calculated three years ago, he/she may well find that at the next review, the maximum income he/she is allowed to draw will be substantially reduced due to a decline in investment markets and the operation of the GAD tables. This income will be further reduced if a Pension Sharing Order is implemented.

If the member is drawing income continuously, all other things being equal, the CETV of his/her pension is bound to decline between the date that it is calculated for negotiations, and the date of implementation of any order.

The author's understanding is that the Inland Revenue does not require that the pension credit member should continue an income withdrawal arrangement after the Pension Sharing Order has been implemented. However, the conditions of the particular policy might only offer this option, or the option to buy an annuity.

The pension debit member might find that his/her fund after implementation is no longer big enough to meet the criteria set by the pension provider for income drawdown to continue after implementation of the order. This could force annuity purchase at a time when the investment market is distressed.

11.6   SMALL SELF-ADMINISTERED PENSION SCHEMES

Implementing a Pension Sharing Order in respect of a SSAS can involve many pitfalls for the unwary.

Transferring out

The actuarial basis used to establish the maximum funding level of a SSAS is, effectively, prescribed, and does not necessarily reflect the basis on which the CETVs will be calculated.

Although the CETV is usually taken as the market value of the member's share of fund, restrictions might apply in some situations. On transfer to a personal pension, restrictions on the CETV might apply for members who are controlling directors, or earn more than the earnings cap, or who are aged more than 45. This restriction does not apply on transfer to a buy-out policy or to an occupational pension scheme, but in such cases the actuary might have to test the CETV against a different limit.

Transfers between pension schemes of the same employer are not restricted, so if it is intended to take a CETV, and one of the above restrictions apply, it might be possible to set up a new scheme to which the pension credit member transfers and becomes the only member.

The nature of the SSAS investments also needs to be considered. It may be that the largest single investment of a SSAS is a single property leased to the sponsoring company. The pension credit member might find it difficult or impossible to organise a transfer in a short period of time. The client might be exposed to a significant investment risk.

As stated at 7.6, a SSAS can invest up to 50 per cent of its assets in the sponsoring company in the form of shares or property. If the transferee takes an external transfer, the effect may be to breach that 50 per cent limit, thus causing penal tax consequences to the SSAS.

Asset apportionment

This was referred to at 7.6. There may be scope for re-apportionment of assets between a husband and a wife who are both members of the SSAS without the need for a Pension Sharing Order. Care is required to ensure that this is not seen to be a method of manipulating the SSAS for tax purposes.

Inland Revenue limits

Pension credits are not tested against the maximum benefits permitted in respect of the pension credit member. What happens in practice is that the maximum benefits of the pension debit member are reduced by the amount of the pension credit. However, care is required where both parties are members of the same pension scheme (which often happens under a SSAS). Unless the rules of the SSAS specifically state that pension credit benefits are payable in addition to the member's own right benefits, the pension credit benefits would be tested against the pension credit member's maximum benefits. Care must be taken here, or the pension credit member could lose part of the pension credit.

Practical issues

The nature of a SSAS means that careful thought is needed. It is not sufficient to get a CETV quotation and then arrange a Pension Sharing Order. The objectives of the client need to be carefully considered. If the intention of the client is to arrange a pension transfer immediately on implementation, this could be frustrated; the client could lose part of the pension share because of the technical operation of the SSAS or because of investment risk.

Beating the Inland Revenue

The author has come across an imaginative idea that involved back-to-back Pension Sharing Orders. The situation was one where the SSAS was overfunded. The only two members were the divorcing couple. The proposal was that the husband would allow a 100 per cent sharing order in favour of the wife. She would not be subject to a test of Inland Revenue limits against the pension credit, so she would be able to transfer all of the assets to another pension arrangement. A Pension Sharing Order in favour of the husband would then be issued against the other arrangement. The husband's idea was that he would then not be tested against Inland Revenue limits in respect of this pension credit. Leading Counsel's opinion was this would be a flagrant breach of the code governing pension schemes and would lead to retrospective removal of the tax-exempt approval of the SSAS.

11.7   EARLY RETIREMENT AND OTHER DISCRETIONARY BENEFITS

This is another tricky area. The Regulations are clear that the courts should base any Pension Sharing Order on the CETV. In the majority of situations, this might not be an unreasonable approach to take. However, in defined benefit schemes actuaries are not able to take into account benefits/options which are payable at the discretion of the trustees, unless the trustees have given instruction that discretionary benefits should be taken into account generally in the calculation of CETVs. It is rare for such an instruction to be given.

Discretionary benefits such as pension increases at a greater value than is promised in the pension scheme rules, or early retirement without penalty, can have significant value, and there may be an established practice of such benefits being awarded. (See in particular police, firefighters and armed services pension schemes.)

In order to bring the value of such benefits to the attention of the courts, it is often necessary to commission an expert witness report from an actuary. This report will set out the principles underlying the calculation of the CETV and contrast this with the value allowing for the discretionary benefit. It could influence the court to award a greater proportion of the CETV to the non-member spouse. Thought has to be given as to whether the cost of commissioning the report and the likelihood of success makes it worthwhile.

11.8 DIVORCES CLOSE TO RETIREMENT AGE

For practical reasons, it is often necessary to rely on CETVs which are somewhat out of date. In current market conditions, this could mean that the CETV that is being used is greater or less than the current CETV. The situation is further compounded by the fact that it could then take a further four months to implement the Pension Sharing Order. At the point of implementation, a new CETV is calculated and the difference in the figure used to reach the settlement and that used to implement the order will crystallise.

Whilst it may be difficult in practice to get round this issue, one has to guard against the member spouse taking action to alter the size of the CETV, or the form of the benefits.

The greatest danger is where a practitioner is acting for the potential pension credit member and the pension debit member opts to retire immediately after a Pension Sharing Order is issued, but before it takes effect. If, for example, the pension arrangement subject to the order is a personal pension, the member could take 25 per cent of the fund as tax-free cash and take one year's pension in advance. Not only would this deplete the fund available for pension sharing, but it could also result in the pension credit member being prevented from using any option to convert part of the fund to tax-free cash (see 3.9).

11.9 MISTAKES AND OVERSIGHTS

Experience has taught the author to treat information from pension scheme administrators with some caution. In one case, information was provided by a reputable organisation setting out the value of a SIPP for one of its clients. The value was quoted at over £1m. Some way down the line, an actuary queried the figure only to be told that it was incorrect and that the true figure was actually closer to £450,000. When provided with CETVs by administrators of defined benefit schemes, it is worth confirming that the figure includes the value of any AVC fund built up by the member. This is frequently overlooked, or is provided separately.

In some funds, in particular with-profit funds, there is a termination penalty should a transfer proceed. It is the amount which would be available for transfer which represents a CETV. If the administrator simply quotes the current fund value, with no allowance for the penalty on transfer, the CETV could be overstated.

The calculation of a CETV from a defined benefit scheme is often delegated by the actuary to a scheme administrator using tailored software and/or factors and worksheets. It is not unknown for information to be input incorrectly or the wrong data used.

This produces a dilemma. Actuaries and other pension specialists are not cheap to employ, but there can be significant risk if specialist knowledge is not employed. Broadly speaking, it will seldom be economic to instruct an actuary where the CETV is less that £250,000 and certainly not if it is below £100,000.

11.10   VALUATION ISSUES

Much ink has been spilled on Thorpe LJ's comments in *Maskell* [2003] 1 FLR 1138 cautioning against comparing the transfer value of a pension which represents a future annuity stream and a portion of future capital on a 'like for like' basis with currently available capital. Bear in mind that the test of 'fairness' requires one to look at the proper division of different classes of assets with different risks attached. Singer J stated the obvious in *F* v. *F* [2003] 1 FLR 847, at para. 14, when he said, 'I very much bear in mind that these pension valuations, whether expressed as CETVs or as a value of a fund held in cash, are for practically all purposes a quite distinct form of currency compared with assets which can be realised for cash which is then freely available'. At para. 15 he states, 'in this manner, the section 25 discretion as to the pension assets can be looked at in isolation, as it were, although always taking into account their nature, value and proposed distribution when standing back to consider how fair and appropriate any proposed order is overall'.

I have always thought that one should distinguish between the value one ascribes to a pension fund in cases where the ultimate resolution is going to involve continuing periodical payments and 'clean break' cases. In the former, it is important to distinguish between the annuity fund and the commutable fund. For example, a husband aged 50 has a pension fund of £300,000; on his retirement, say, £75,000 can be commuted tax-free; £225,000 will be available to purchase a taxable annuity. At a broad estimate, his average tax rate may be about 20 per cent and so it seems right to me that £45,000 should be deducted from the value of the non-commutable element. In any event, it is a fund that should be set on one side in looking at the parties' assets as it is that fund that is going to support maintenance post-retirement.

So far as clean break orders are concerned, I have discussed the correct approach to valuation with Singer J and he agreed that the gross value of the member's pension fund should be brought into account. The court is looking at the capital and other resources that each spouse will have to generate an income that will enable them both to stand on their own two feet. After deducting liabilities, it only nets down those resources to allow for CGT on their realisation, so as to compare the gross income that each party can generate. To value the member spouse's pension annuity fund net of tax would be to treat it differently from all other capital resources that the spouses have. Support for this view can also be found in the judgment of Bennett J in *Norris* v. *Norris* [2003] 1 FLR 1142, [2003] 2 FLR 1124, CA at para. 72, and in the judgment of Nicholas Mostyn QC in *GW* v. *RW* [2003] 2 FLR 108 at para. 20 when he said it would be wrong to discount the husband's individual retirement account (a US pension scheme) funds for tax.

11.11 EXPERTS

The experts involved are:

- family lawyer;
- pensions lawyer;
- actuary;
- fund manager;
- IFA.

All have different, overlapping roles. None can do the job of the other four. All are nonetheless prone to 'having a go' at the job of the other four. The most likely combination is that of a family lawyer and an actuary. Some are lucky to have in-house pensions lawyers working in their employment department who can be of enormous assistance, but actuaries do tend to have a sufficiently wide understanding of the law and practice relating to pensions, plus an excellent grasp of the financial points, and can be invaluable. In the author's experience, IFAs do not have the same level of knowledge as actuaries. Only those that have a G60 qualification can, as well as actuaries, advise on what a client should do with their pension share. Solicitors cannot. For a solicitor to so advise is a breach of the Financial Services and Markets Act 2000.

CHAPTER 12

Digest of pensions cases

12.1 GENERAL

This chapter will cover, almost exclusively, the more important cases that have come before the courts under MCA 1973, ss.25B to 25D and the Welfare Reform and Pensions Act 1999. These are, of course, the attachment provisions enacted by Pensions Act (PA) 1995, s.166(1) and the Pension Sharing Orders introduced by the WRPA 1999.

As the reader will know (and this is of course only a summary), after the PA 1995 for the first time Pension Attachment Orders could be made; although they were made against a respondent to an application and the involvement of the pension provider was ancillary, they were effective against pension providers. Also for the first time, the court was given a statutory power to order a party with pension rights to exercise the whole or part of that party's right to commute to a lump sum and the court could attach part or all of the lump sum. There was also power to attach pension annuities, via a periodical payments order, which became effective when that pension annuity came to be paid. A lump sum available to a party with pension rights was attachable by way of a lump sum or sums order, and/or a secured provision order. A lump sum order could also now be made in respect of any sum payable on the death of a partner to a marriage whose estate might otherwise obtain that sum.

The two principal decisions under pension attachment law are *T* v. *T* [1998] 1 FLR 1072 and *Burrow* v. *Burrow* [1999] 1 FLR 508. Both are first instance decisions. For the sake of brevity, the author will not set out the detailed facts of the case (the reader is well advised to cast an eye over the head note, if not read the whole of the judgments) but set out the guidelines and general ratio of each decision.

12.2   *T* v. *T*

From *T* v. *T* the following general points of principle emerge.

The amended MCA 1973 does not require the court to compensate for pension loss automatically. What it does do is to oblige the court to consider first if an order for periodical payments, secured provision or lump sum is appropriate, and then to consider how pension considerations should affect the terms of any such order.

It might well be that having considered the pension legislation, the court will decide not to exercise its powers at all under MCA 1973, ss.25B to 25D.

The court may well be slow to make any orders at all allocating pension benefits where the parties are not close to retirement. This is because:

(a)   orders relating to far into the future may really not provide much eventual security;

(b)   orders for earmarking are, even in the case of deferred lump sums, variable in future applications;

(c)   it may be safest from the point of view of the court to wait until a husband had retired so as to ensure that the correct order is made;

(d)   the remedies available under the Inheritance (Provision for Family and Dependants) Act 1975, if the wife remains still dependent on her husband post-retirement, may well mean that there is no need to make immediate orders, especially where the parties are in their 30s or 40s.

Another important feature of *T* v. *T* is that court stated that it did not obtain much benefit from actuarial calculations designed to demonstrate each party's notional share in the future income stream, expressed now as capital, and also did not obtain much assistance from the figure calculated to show the loss of a dependant's pension after the death of the respective spouse. This, however, does not mean that such calculations will never be helpful and the author's view is that such calculations may represent a valuable tool, and certainly a guide; whilst not denying for a moment that their specificity may well be deceptive if relied upon too heavily. Actuarial calculations may certainly help in a broad-brush way to determine the loss of benefit, where that is a calculation which needs to be made.

12.3   *BURROW* v. *BURROW*

From *Burrow* v. *Burrow*, where the lump sum payable by way of commutation was attached, as opposed to *T* v. *T* where it was not, it becomes clear that the way the court will approach allocating benefits under MCA 1973, ss.25B to 25D, is primarily subordinate to the way the court will first approach all the other assets. Pension annuities now seem unlikely to be attached when the date for their payment is far in the future. Different considerations apply to capital: remarriage will not terminate an earmarking order made against capital within a scheme. An annuity might not be available for 15 years but an order against capital now – in effect an order that the husband was to pay half the maximum lump sum on his retirement – might properly be made, reflecting as it might past contributions of capital. The court will also be more ready to make orders allocating benefits payable on death now, so as to provide certainty for dependants in the future. This is certainly the case where the trustees of a pension fund have a legal discretion to ignore a nomination as to the payment of a lump sum payable on death. Following *White* v. *White*, it seems likely that the court will be far readier to attach the lump sum a person with pension rights is eligible to receive, and will in reality start from the position of saying that if such an order ought to be made, it will be (in the case of a long marriage, where the parties have made an equal contribution) from a position of an equal split. All this, however, assumes that for one reason or another it will not be possible to make a Pension Sharing Order under the WRPA 1999.

12.4   *H* v. *H*

A case (but an important one) decided well before the PA 1995 varied the MCA 1973, is *H* v. *H* [1993] 2 FLR 335. Relevant principles that arise from this case are as follows:

- first look at the value of what has been earned during the period of cohabitation;
- secondly, look at the prospective value of what might be earned over the period after separation but before retirement;
- thirdly, do not compensate over-much, or possibly not at all, a party who has an inferior pension building capacity (often a wife) to make up for the fact that her ability to amass pension benefits in the future may be inferior to that of her husband.

Given that the ages of the parties in this case were 39 years and 42 years respectively, this case is, in the author's view, very useful in considering the pension rights of couples in their 30s or early 40s. The weight to be given to the approach taken in the judgment (at pp. 343 and 344) to the disparity in the spouses' ability to accumulate pension rights over time post-separation obviously diminishes the older the spouses are and the closer they are to retirement. One can particularly envisage a court applying the passage stating that the relevant contributions are those made during cohabitation within marriage to a case involving the termination of a second marriage.

12.5 *MASKELL* v. *MASKELL*

A decision that was not widely known when it was initially reported but which has now appeared at [2003] 1 FLR 1138 is the important case of *Maskell* v. *Maskell*. This case, a Court of Appeal decision, is of importance because it makes plain that the court must not equate money in a pension fund with money that may be derived from the sale of an asset now, even if the sale of such an asset may be difficult. In particular, a pension represents, usually, as to 75 per cent of it, only a future income stream, which will be subject to tax at whatever rate is prevailing; the remaining 25 per cent of it will represent only a deferred, potential capital benefit (the deferred capital benefit may not always be paid when one remembers the recent difficulties of certain pension providers). Accordingly, the practitioner must guard against the heresy of any opponent attempting to bring into account a CETV as if it was potential ready money (but see also 11.10).

12.6 CASES UNDER THE WRPA 1999

The WRPA 1999 brought in for the first time a Pension Sharing Order. Under this legislation there have so far been relatively few cases. In *S* v. *S* (Rescission of Decree Nisi: Pension Sharing Provision) [2002] 1 FLR 457, the court by consent was prepared to allow a decree nisi to be set aside so as to allow fresh proceedings to be launched (brought as they needed to be after 1 December 2000) so as to confer a jurisdiction to make a Pension Sharing Order. It is apparent, however, from the case of *Rye* v. *Rye* [2002] EWHC 956 (Fam), [2002] 2 FLR 1981, and also from *H* v. *H* [2002] EWHC 767 (Fam) FD, [2002] 2 FLR 116, that if one party refuses consent to the decree nisi being rescinded in order to mobilise the court's power to make a Pension Sharing Order, then the court will not be prepared to rescind the decree nisi.

As is apparent, the date when proceedings are begun is crucial to the operation of the pension sharing jurisdiction. In *W* v. *W* [2002] EWHC 1826 Fam, [2002] 2 FLR 1225, it was held that, even though a cross petition was launched in February 2001, when the original petition was filed on 24 August 2000, and an answer filed on 26 September 2000, the court did not have jurisdiction to make a Pension Sharing Order. The divorce proceedings constituted one set of proceedings (begun in August 2000) and a cross petition could not constitute separate proceedings in the sense referred to in Welfare Reform and Pensions Act 1999, s.83(3)(a), despite the fact that it was a fresh cause of action.

12.7   *FIELD* v. *FIELD*

An interesting and unusual recent case (on enforcement against pension assets and the use of injunctions and receivers in this regard) is *Field* v. *Field* [2003] 1 FLR 376. The facts were unusual, and again for the sake of brevity will not be set out. The following principles may derived from the judgment.

Whilst, as a matter of law, assets in a pension scheme might be made subject to a charging order, if the provisions of the scheme do not give an immediate beneficial entitlement in assets to a party and/or the scheme prohibits the asset being charged, then the court (irrespective of the contempt of the party who has failed to obey orders/undertakings to pay instalments of a lump sum under an existing ancillary relief order) will not override this.

An injunction could be granted under the Supreme Court Act 1971 as an aid to the court's established procedure for enforcement of a judgment against a pension, but not as a free-standing enforcement procedure in its own right. This is irrespective of the width of Supreme Court Act 1971, s.37, and the fact that a party is in breach of an order to pay £500,000. The legal concept that methods of enforcement are usually complementary, and that the strength of the injunctive jurisdiction is that it has always helped where statute leaves off and subsumes that within itself, does not seem to apply in enforcement against pension assets.

A receiver could be appointed in aid of execution of a judgment against a pension scheme but only if the sums payable to the husband under the scheme were capable of being assigned. The question whether a receiver ever has power to elect a lump sum from a pension on a particular date remains open.

This was a case to which PA 1995, s.166, did not apply. Was there an independent right to compel a husband by way of injunction to elect commutation of his pension on a particular date in the future, irrespective of s.166? The court decided in effect that, because no one had apparently thought of doing this before (giving rise to a need to enact the powers in s.166), the power to compel a husband to elect to take a lump sum commutation on a fixed date by way of injunction, separate and apart from s.166, simply did not exist.

12.8 *RE NUNN*

The complications that bankruptcy causes where pension funds are a part of the assets of the bankrupt's estate are fiendish. They are nowhere better illustrated than in the recent case of *Re Nunn* [2004] 1 FLR 1123, an appeal against a first instance decision to a Deputy High Court Judge of the Chancery Division. Here, the court held that a 1994 consent order, under which a husband would pay to a wife one-half of the contingent lump sums he would receive under various pension policies, were not exempted by Insolvency Act 1986, ss.283(3), (5), and that they vested in the trustee in bankruptcy. The court held that in ancillary relief proceedings, it lacked jurisdiction to make an order for the payment of these lump sums in any form that created an equitable interest or security. The section apparently had no application. Apparently, what the original order had done was to assign *not* the right to be paid half the lump sum in accordance with the policy, but rather *a half interest in the fund created by the payments of the lump sums.* On these facts there was no exclusion from the rule that the assets vest in the trustee on bankruptcy, because the ancillary relief order apparently did not create property 'held by the bankrupt on trust for another person', nor was the property 'subject to the rights of any person whether as a secured creditor of the bankrupt or otherwise'. The court also rejected the finding of the judge that the assignment of the rights to the capital under MCA 1973, s.23, had the same effect as a specifically enforceable contract and created an immediate equitable interest. The court held that a strict construction of the ancillary relief court's powers in relation to lump sum orders meant that it had no power to do what it had purported to do, and surprisingly that the husband would have been entitled to have the order set aside. (But on what terms?) It is likely that the operation of WRPA 1999, ss.11, 12, would, if the matter were to happen now, exclude the pension rights from vesting in the bankrupt's estate. The moral of the story appears to be that a practitioner ought immediately to take expert specialist bankruptcy advice when a trustee attacks an order or a transaction.

12.9   GRAVE FINANCIAL HARDSHIP

As a result of the court's power to make a Pension Sharing Order, it is now extremely difficult to see how a loss of pension rights could be used to prevent a decree of divorce under MCA 1973, s.1(2)(e) on the grounds of grave financial hardship. Accordingly, all the cases on this topic will now need to be read with caution. Obviously, if for one reason or another pension sharing is not available (most likely if a scheme is overseas) such a defence is still likely to be available.

12.10   PENSION SHARING POST-*WHITE*

It is worth remembering what Lord Nicholls said about pre-acquired capital and considering whether, particularly in a second marriage, where the husband has built up a pension fund prior to a marriage, the court will look differently in the circumstances of a case at that part of the fund that was acquired pre-marriage from the fund that accrued post-marriage.

12.11   WHY DIVORCE?

In certain cases, particularly where the member spouse is already drawing a pension, the best solution may be to stay married or merely have a judicial separation with an order attaching a percentage of the member spouse's pension in favour of the non-member spouse, who will then be the widow(er) on the member spouse's death and draw the widow's/widower's pension.

CHAPTER 13

Civil Partnership Act 2004

13.1 GENERAL

The Civil Partnership Act 2004, which has had quite a difficult passage through Parliament, will, once it is brought into force, enable same sex couples, who are not already married or registered civil partners, to register as civil partners.

At the time of writing the Bill provides that on the breakdown of the relationship, a civil partner can apply for a separation order, a dissolution order or, on the ground the civil partnership is void or voidable, a nullity order, and a presumption of death order.

A dissolution order cannot be sought before the end of one year from the date of the formation of the civil partnership.

As in divorce, every dissolution, nullity or presumption of death order is initially conditional and cannot be made final for six weeks from the maturing of the conditional order.

13.2 GROUNDS FOR DISSOLUTION

The grounds for dissolution are:

- unreasonable behaviour;
- two years' separation and consent;
- five years' separation with no consent; and
- two years' desertion.

The same defence that dissolution will result in grave financial or other hardship and it would be wrong in all the circumstances to dissolve the civil partnership applies in five year separation cases as in divorce.

Likewise there is provision for protection of the respondent in two year separation and consent cases that echoes MCA 1973, s.10.

13.3 FINANCIAL RELIEF IN CONNECTION WITH DISSOLUTION, NULLITY OR SEPARATION

The full range of financial provision, property adjustment and Pension Sharing Orders are available, only taking effect in the case of dissolution or nullity cases when the final order is made. Similar discretionary guidelines apply as under MCA 1973, s.25, with provision for a clean break.

As in divorce, it is only on making a dissolution or nullity order that the court can make a Pension Sharing Order. A Pension Attachment Order can be made on a separation order as well as on making a dissolution or nullity order.

The wording and definitions are the same as under the WRPA 1999 amendments to the MCA 1973.

The pension attachment provisions echo those on divorce. If a pension is attached as part of a periodical payments order, the order will end on the payer's death, on the payer entering into another civil partnership or marrying.

A Pension Sharing Order can be made to effect a 'clean break' on discharging or varying a periodical payments order or a secured periodical payments order made after dissolution of a civil partnership.

The provisions for varying or appealing Pension Sharing Orders echo those on divorce.

There are mirror provisions to MCA 1973, s.37, for injunctions to restrain dispositions intended to defeat an application for financial relief.

There are mirror provisions to seek financial provision after an overseas dissolution or annulment of a civil partnership or a legal separation of a civil partnership overseas, even if the date of dissolution, annulment or legal separation is earlier than the date on which the relevant part of the Act comes into force.

CHAPTER 14

Personal insolvency

Roger Elford and James Hyne

14.1 GENERAL

An individual may be declared bankrupt by one of two methods; upon his/her own petition or alternatively upon the petition of a creditor (usually following service of a statutory demand and presentation of a bankruptcy petition to the court in respect of an undisputed debt of more than £750).

Bankruptcy law has seen significant change over a relatively short period of time; the Bankruptcy Act 1914 remained in force relatively unscathed for over 70 years until the government commissioned the most wide-reaching consultation in respect of personal and corporate insolvency culminating in the Cork Report (*Insolvency Law and Practice*, Report of the Insolvency Law Review Committee (1982)). Consequently, fundamental and wide-reaching reforms to the law in this area were introduced by the Insolvency Act (IA) 1986.

14.2 FURTHER CHANGES TO THE LAW OF PERSONAL INSOLVENCY

Primarily in response to a need for fundamental reform of corporate insolvency, the Enterprise Act (EA) 2002, which came into force on 15 September 2003, introduced further significant changes to the law of personal insolvency with effect from 1 April 2004.

The fundamental concepts, which will be considered below, have not changed through the introduction of the EA 2002, although a brief analysis of the reforms introduced is worthwhile. In summary, the IA 1986 'one size fits all' regime whereby a first bankruptcy would be automatically discharged after a mandatory three-year period (regardless of the size of the debt(s) incurred by the bankrupt) has been abolished. For all bankruptcies commenced after 1 April 2004, a bankrupt will be discharged after a *maximum* of 12 months but it is anticipated that this period may be reduced to as little as three months if the Official Receiver can complete his initial enquiries and is satisfied that no further investigations are required into the bankrupt's affairs.

For 'culpable' bankrupts, a bankruptcy restriction order may now be imposed (or a bankruptcy restriction undertaking may be given) whereby the bankrupt will be subject to certain statutory restrictions upon his/her conduct and business dealings for a period of between two and 15 years. IA 1986, s.281A and Sched. 4A (as inserted by EA 2002, s.257 and Sched. 20) provide a non-exhaustive list of certain activities or behaviour which may lead to the imposition of a bankruptcy restriction order (or the giving of a bankruptcy restriction undertaking) which include excessive contributions to the bankrupt's pension arrangements (see Sched. 4A, para. 2(2)(e)).

Such excessive contributions are also voidable pursuant to IA 1986, s.342A, as a bankrupt may have sought to put his/her assets beyond the reach of his/her creditors by paying excessive sums towards his/her pension arrangements which may then be excluded from the bankrupt's estate if the pension benefit in question will not otherwise 'vest' in his/her trustee in bankruptcy pursuant to IA 1986, s.306. In this regard, pension scheme trustees or providers must comply with any request for information by a trustee in bankruptcy within nine weeks from the date the request is received. This nine week time limit is imposed by Occupational and Personal Pension Schemes (Bankruptcy) (No. 2) Regulations 2002, SI 2002/836, reg. 10(1). If it is found that excessive pension contributions have been made, a restoration order may be made by the court, and pursuant to reg. 8 of SI 2002/836, the pension scheme trustees or providers must comply with the restoration order within 17 weeks from the date of service of the order.

It is to be noted that the fundamental principle of the vesting of a bankrupt's property in his/her trustee in bankruptcy pursuant to IA 1986, s.306 has not changed.

14.3   VESTING OF THE BANKRUPT'S ESTATE

Insolvency Act 1986, s.306 states:

> (1) The bankrupt's estate shall vest in the trustee immediately on his appointment taking effect or, in the case of the official receiver, on becoming his trustee.

(2) Where any property which is, or is to be, comprised in the bankrupt's estate vests in the trustee (whether under this section or under any other provision of this Part), it shall so vest without any conveyance, assignment or transfer.

In simple terms, any property the bankrupt owns automatically vests in the trustee in bankruptcy upon the making of a bankruptcy order.

Much case law and authority has arisen in respect of the question of what constitutes 'property' and therefore will vest in the trustee in bankruptcy as opposed to 'personal' rights which fall outside of the bankruptcy estate. Tenancy rights, insurance policies, compensation for personal injury, claims for unfair dismissal and future royalty payments have all come before the court in order to decide whether such categories constitute 'property' for the purposes of IA 1986, s.306. Pension rights have been no less subject to similar analysis in the context of vesting pursuant to s.306.

Whether rights to pensions form part of the estate or can be excluded from vesting in the individual's trustee in bankruptcy had been widely debated and contested until statutory intervention in the form of the Welfare Reform and Pensions Act 1999. These new provisions sought to clarify the law relating to pension rights of individuals who are declared bankrupt.

14.4 BANKRUPTCIES COMMENCING PRIOR TO 29 MAY 2000

Following the Court of Appeal's decision in *Jones* v. *Patel and London Borough of Brent* [1999] BPIR 509, it became settled law that, upon the incidence of the bankruptcy of an individual (and in the absence of an effective forfeiture clause in the scheme's trust deed: see 14.6 onwards), the individual's rights under an occupational pension scheme vest automatically in his/her trustee in bankruptcy.

In *Jones*, the court held that, because the legal right of the individual to compel the payment of the pension scheme was vested in that individual prior to him/her becoming bankrupt, this right was a chose in action and therefore 'property' of the bankrupt for the purposes of IA 1986, s.436. Accordingly, the right to the benefits from Mr Jones' pension policies vested in his trustee in bankruptcy, save to the extent that they were derived from or related to post-bankruptcy contributions or employment.

The legal position relating to bankrupts' rights under retirement annuity contracts (RACs) and personal pension plans was clarified soon after. In *Dennison* v. *Krasner*; *Lesser* v. *Lawrence* [2000] 3 WLR 720, the Court of Appeal held that, whether or not such arrangements contained an anti-alienation provision (as such plans are required to contain in order to qualify for tax approval), the bankrupt's rights constituted his 'property' and therefore vested in his trustee in bankruptcy. By contrast with a restriction on alienation in an occupational pension scheme, such a provision in a retirement annuity or personal pension was held to be nothing more than an attempt to contract out of the bankruptcy legislation (which, in turn, was contrary to public policy).

The only exception to these general principles concerned 'guaranteed minimum pensions' and 'protected rights', payable (in lieu of state benefits) by occupational and personal pension schemes that contract out of SERPS and its successor, S2P. These benefits were protected from forfeiture by Pension Schemes Act (PSA) 1993, s.159(5), which provided, until its repeal as from 6 April 2002 and replacement with more comprehensive provisions (see 14.6), that no such rights would pass to a trustee in bankruptcy.

IA 1986, s.306 provides that the bankrupt's estate (comprising all of his/her property save for a number of small exceptions) will vest in his/her trustee in bankruptcy 'without any conveyance, assignment or transfer'. Once it was established that (subject to these limited exceptions) a bankrupt's right under an occupational or personal pension scheme could be properly defined as being property of the bankrupt, pension scheme trustees or providers who delayed or refused to recognise the trustee in bankruptcy's rights were often threatened with proceedings for contempt of court pursuant to IA 1986, s.312(4), which provides that:

> if any person without reasonable excuse fails to comply with any obligation imposed by this section, he is guilty of a contempt of court and liable to be punished accordingly (in addition to any other punishments to which he may be subject).

As alluded to above, an important factor to consider when looking at the position prior to 29 May 2000 is the existence (or otherwise) of forfeiture provisions in pension scheme trust deeds and rules. This is considered below in 14.6. A further consideration, which applies equally to pre- and post-May 2000 bankruptcies, is the extent to which a trustee in bankruptcy will be bound by an ancillary relief order that was made prior to the incidence of bankruptcy. See below 14.8 which addresses this and related issues.

14.5   BANKRUPTCIES COMMENCING ON OR AFTER 29 MAY 2000

The position is now governed primarily by WRPA 1999, s.11, which was hastily brought into effect by the then DSS in order to counteract the effect of the judgment in *Lesser* v. *Lawrence*. It operates so as to exclude certain 'approved' pension schemes from the bankrupt's estate, subject to the clawback provisions of IA 1986, ss.342A to 342C. The 'approved' pension schemes in question are tax-approved personal or occupational pension schemes (including RACs), and annuities purchased with the proceeds of any such arrangements under the 'open market option' which allows pensioners to choose by whom their ultimate benefits are provided.

The provisions applying in respect of *unapproved* (or top-up) pension arrangements are governed by WRPA 1999, s.12, which was brought into effect on 6 April 2002 along with the majority of the Act's other provisions. The position in respect of these benefits is set out below. It is important to note, however, that whilst s.12 only applies as from that later date, it would appear to catch all bankruptcies as at that date; and therefore, by contrast to s.11, would not be limited to those that commenced on or after 29 May 2000.

The basic principle is that rights under unapproved pension arrangements (as defined in WRPA 1999, s.12(3)) will fall into the bankrupt's estate. However, if (which is possible but would be unusual) they constitute the bankrupt's sole or main means of pension provision, a bankrupt may be able to protect his/her rights under an unapproved scheme in one of two ways under SI 2002/836.

In order to benefit from this protection:

(a)   the bankrupt may, within nine weeks from the date on which his/her pension rights vested in the trustee in bankruptcy, enter into a 'qualifying agreement' with the trustee in bankruptcy whereby the unapproved pension rights are excluded from the bankruptcy; alternatively

(b)   the bankrupt may, within 13 weeks from the date on which his/her pension rights vested in the trustee in bankruptcy, apply to the court for an 'exclusion order' to the effect that unapproved pension rights fall outside of the bankruptcy estate.

If the bankrupt makes a material non-disclosure, the trustee in bankruptcy may revoke the qualifying agreement. In such circumstances the bankrupt will have a shorter period of 30 days in which to apply for an exclusion order. Both the 13 week and 30 day periods referred to above may be extended at the discretion of the court upon the bankrupt's application.

In determining whether to make an exclusion order in respect of the unapproved pension rights, the trustee in bankruptcy or court will look at the bankrupt's future needs and the adequacy of his/her likely income from other pension arrangements.

14.6   FORFEITURE PROVISIONS IN PENSION SCHEMES

6 April 2002 onwards

In the past, many pension schemes contained clauses which purported to forfeit (or allow the forfeiture of) an individual's pension benefits upon the making of a bankruptcy order in respect of that individual. Since 6 April 2002, any clause in a pension scheme trust deed or rules that seeks to forfeit a person's rights under that scheme by reference to his/her bankruptcy has been unlawful, in respect (it is considered, because WRPA 1999, s.14 makes no reference to the date of presentation of the bankruptcy petition) of bankruptcies commencing both pre- and post-6 April 2002.

WRPA 1999, s.14 inserts a new s.159A into the PSA 1993, which now provides that a person's rights under a personal pension scheme cannot be forfeited by reference to his/her bankruptcy (s.159A(1)). Section 14 also deletes Pensions Act (PA) 1995, s.92(2)(b), thereby ostensibly outlawing forfeiture provisions in occupational pension schemes too (s.159A(3)). These provisions prevent the forfeiture under such arrangements of a member's entire pension benefit, and not simply the 'guaranteed minimum pensions' and 'protected rights' that were deemed outside the scope of the bankruptcy estate by the now-repealed s.159(5) (see 14.4).

Difficulties may nonetheless arise in practice, despite the ostensibly clear language of the statute. Where a bankruptcy arising from a petition presented before 29 May 2000 is only notified to the pension scheme provider after 6 April 2002, the pension will not have fallen outside the member's bankruptcy estate but the ability to forfeit it will no longer exist either. At best this gives rise to inconsistencies and at worst is open to abuse, and as a result it is not necessarily clear that s.14 should properly render forfeiture clauses ineffective in respect of bankruptcy petitions presented pre-29 May 2000. However, until clarified by the courts, the position will remain subject to some uncertainty.

Position prior to 6 April 2002: occupational pension schemes

The position relating to forfeiture provisions in occupational pension scheme trust deeds before 6 April 2002 has been the subject of numerous cases before the courts which have examined the validity of various types of forfeiture clause.

The two leading cases in this area in relation to occupational pension schemes are the 2001 Chancery Division decision in the case of *Money Markets International Stock Brokers Ltd (in liquidation)* v. *London Stock Exchange and another* [2002] 1 WLR 1150 and the 1999 decision in the case of *In Re Trusts of the Scientific Investment Pension Plan* [1998] 3 WLR 1191 (often referred to by the name of *Kemble* v. *Hicks*), where the effectiveness of forfeiture clauses under occupational pension schemes was examined. In *Scientific Investments*, Rattee J considered various cases that had established sets of rules for the construction of valid forfeiture and alienation clauses in pension trusts deeds. He set out by way of summary the legal position in respect of various forfeiture provisions in the following way:

(a) A forfeiture clause purporting to forfeit an absolute interest in possession in the event of alienation will be void;

(b) So will be such a clause which purports similarly to forfeit a life or other limited interest in possession which is not, on the true construction of the instrument creating it, made determinable in the same events as those in which the forfeiture is expressed to operate.

(c) On the other hand, there is nothing objectionable about such a forfeiture clause which purports to defeat a future interest in the event of purported alienation before it falls into possession, or to create a gift over in the event in which an income interest in possession is, on the true construction of the trust instrument, expressed to be determinable.

If a forfeiture clause purports to apply both to interests in possession within (a) or (b) above and to future or determinable interests within (c) above, it will be wholly void, even as to interests within (c) above as to which it would have been valid if limited to interests within that class.

Consequently a clause will be effective, if it defeats a future interest by means of alienation before it falls into the possession of the member. Each case will depend upon the wording of the forfeiture provision in the particular trust deed concerned but the courts have determined that once an individual becomes absolutely entitled to the benefits under a pension scheme, in the event of his/her bankruptcy, that interest will vest in the individual's trustee in bankruptcy.

In cases where an occupational pension scheme trust deed contained a valid forfeiture clause, upon the valid forfeiture (prior to April 2002) of the member's pension entitlement, the assets representing that entitlement usually became held by the pension scheme trustees under a discretionary trust for a class of beneficiaries which often included the bankrupt, his/her spouse and any close dependants. In such cases, the trustees of the pension scheme could then apply the forfeited entitlement in favour of the people within these classes at their absolute discretion, thus avoiding any potential argument by the trustee in bankruptcy that the assets of the scheme or any part of them were vested in him/her pursuant to IA 1986, s.306.

Position prior to 6 April 2002: personal pension schemes

By contrast, and in the absence of a valid forfeiture clause in the policy concerned, benefits under personal pension schemes (and rights under RACs) vested in the individual's trustee in bankruptcy prior to April 2002. Accordingly, there was often no need for a trustee in bankruptcy to seek an income payments order in respect of personal pension benefits which vested in the bankrupt's estate and became available for the benefit of the bankrupt's creditors.

The position if the personal pension scheme does contain a forfeiture clause is, however, not clear and yet to be tested in court. The decisions in *Lesser* v. *Lawrence*; *Dennison* v. *Krasner* (see 14.4) concerned more general anti-alienation provisions, and did not consider what the position would have been had the policies in question also contained a forfeiture clause. It is arguable that the same principle – the ability to contract out of the bankruptcy regime is contrary to public policy – should apply. However, personal pension scheme providers may be inclined to take a different view, particularly when it is the validity of one of their own forfeiture clauses (and their power as pension provider to exercise it) that is being called into question.

14.7 PENSIONS IN PAYMENT

The position with regard to pension benefits that actually come into payment, whether from an occupational or a personal pension scheme, is less straightforward. Ultimately, it draws together the analysis relating both to the vesting of a bankrupt's rights in his/her trustee in bankruptcy and to the validity of forfeiture clauses, considered above in 14.3 to 14.6.

Pre-April 2002 regime

Leaving aside post-bankruptcy contributions (see 14.4), it depends upon whether the benefits in question fell into the bankrupt's estate. If so (for example because there was no valid forfeiture clause), they thereby became available to his/her creditors. Accordingly, there will have been no need for a trustee in bankruptcy to seek an income payments order pursuant to IA 1986, s.310: see, e.g., *Rowe* v. *Saunders* [2002] EWCA Civ 242.

If by contrast the pension scheme rules did contain a valid forfeiture clause, the pension scheme trustees or provider will have been able to forfeit the bankrupt's pension to prevent it vesting in the bankruptcy estate. If the bankrupt's pension was forfeited in this way, it was common for it to be paid to the bankrupt anyway under the trustees' or provider's discretionary powers. If that was (and is) the case, a trustee in bankruptcy was (and is) then able to apply to the court for an income payments order pursuant to IA 1986, s.310, against both the lump sum and the annual pension being paid from the scheme. Such an order would of course be subject to the protections afforded by s.310, and hence this result might not be as draconian from the individual's perspective as would have been the case had his/her pension rights actually vested in his/her trustee in bankruptcy.

Pension benefits in payment: the new regime

Insofar as the new regime is concerned, similar principles apply. As we have seen, from 6 April 2002, provisions within pension schemes which attempt to circumvent bankruptcy law by seeking to forfeit pension rights upon bankruptcy are of no effect, pursuant to WRPA 1999, s.14 (which inserts a new s.159A to this effect into the PSA 1993). Section 159A(1) provides that an individual's rights under a personal pension scheme cannot be forfeited by reference to his/her bankruptcy. Furthermore, the provisions of the PA 1995 which expressly permitted the forfeiture of occupational pension rights on bankruptcy (see s.92(2)(b)) are rendered ineffective by the new PSA 1993, s.159A(3).

Pension benefits will therefore be excluded from the bankrupt's estate, but still susceptible to an income payments order under IA 1986, s.310 or alternatively an income payments undertaking as introduced from 1 April 2004 by the EA 2002.

14.8 ANCILLARY RELIEF ORDERS MADE PRIOR TO THE INCIDENCE OF BANKRUPTCY

Earmarking in divorce cases was introduced by the PA 1995 (the particular provisions of which came into force on 1 August 1996) and is a term used to describe special attachment orders that the court may make. The effect of an earmarking order is that the pension remains vested in the sole name of the individual member but the occupational scheme's trustees or the personal pension provider is/are then obliged to make payments to the former spouse in accordance with the court's order when the member's benefits become payable.

In the event that a pension scheme member with benefits that are subject to an earmarking order becomes bankrupt pursuant to a petition presented on or after 29 May 2000, then WRPA 1999, s.11 will apply. None of the rights under a tax-approved pension scheme to which the earmarking order applies will be included in the bankruptcy estate. Conversely, in those cases where the bankruptcy petition was presented prior to 29 May 2000, it is suggested that the rights that are the subject of the earmarking order will vest in the bankrupt's trustee in bankruptcy, unless a valid forfeiture clause existed in the pension scheme concerned. Should a former spouse (in whose benefit an earmarking order has been made) be made bankrupt, it is suggested that – irrespective of the date on which the petition was presented – the pension right would not fall into his/her estate or thereby be available to his/her trustee in bankruptcy, other than by means of an income payments order under IA 1986, s.310.

Pension Sharing Orders (discussed in detail in Chapter 3) are only available in divorce and nullity proceedings which commenced on or after 1 December 2000. With WRPA 1999, s.11 having come into force by this time, there are unlikely to be many cases where a member's rights that are subject to a Pension Sharing Order will vest in his/her trustee in bankruptcy. Insofar as a former spouse who becomes bankrupt is concerned, where a petition for his/her bankruptcy was presented on or after 29 May 2000 then a Pension Sharing Order made under an approved pension scheme will be protected under WRPA 1999, s.11 and the benefits will not fall into the hands of his/her trustee in bankruptcy. If the petition was presented prior to 29 May 2000, it is suggested that (in the absence of an effective forfeiture clause) his/her pension share will, by contrast, fall into his/her estate for bankruptcy purposes.

14.9 REMEDIES AVAILABLE TO A TRUSTEE IN BANKRUPTCY IN THE EVENT OF EXCESSIVE CONTRIBUTIONS

The one caveat to the situation described above (and this will also apply to all forms of order or arrangement in divorce or judicial separation proceedings) will be in circumstances where a trustee in bankruptcy considers that there may have been excessive contributions into the pension fund by the bankrupt prior to his/her bankruptcy and, accordingly, that there may be a possibility of the spouse of the bankrupt receiving the benefit of the bankrupt's excessive contributions. The trustee in bankruptcy may seek to claw back any such overpayments for the benefit of the bankrupt's creditors.

WRPA 1999, s.15, substitutes a new set of provisions in IA 1986, ss.342A to 342C in respect of excessive pensions contributions made by a person who has been made bankrupt.

Where a trustee in bankruptcy is of the view that, prior to his/her being made bankrupt, that individual made contributions which are considered to be excessive, the trustee in bankruptcy may apply to the court for an order under s.342A that the position be restored to what it would have been had the excessive contributions not been made. Under s.342A(2), the court may make such an order if it is satisfied that the rights under the pension arrangement concerned are to any extent, and whether directly or indirectly, the 'fruits of relevant contributions', and that the making of any of the relevant contributions ('the excessive contributions') has unfairly prejudiced the bankrupt individual's creditors.

However, it is suggested that it is not the former spouse, but the bankrupt member him/herself, against whom the trustee in bankruptcy may proceed in order to recover 'excessive contributions' that are now represented by the former spouse's rights pursuant to a Pension Sharing Order. Furthermore, this would appear to be the case whether the former spouse's rights have been satisfied by an 'external transfer' to another arrangement, or by an 'internal transfer' of his/her pension credit within the scheme. The legislation deems any excessive contributions from which the former spouse is now benefiting to have been made to the bankrupt member's portion of the shared pension, and accordingly allows the court to order that they – along with all other excessive contributions – be recovered from the bankrupt member's pension rights. The former spouse's pension share is thereby, it appears, protected from diminution as a result of any excessive contributions having been made to his/her pension arrangement by their ex-spouse before their bankruptcy.

However, it remains unclear whether, if the member's rights are exhausted, a trustee in bankruptcy may then proceed against the former spouse in order to recover the remaining pecuniary advantage of the member's excessive contributions.

In determining whether pension contributions could be considered to be excessive, the court is directed under s.342A(6) to consider whether any of the contributions were made for the purposes of putting assets beyond the reach of the individual's creditors or any of them, and whether the total amount of any contributions were of an amount which was excessive in view of the individual's circumstances when those contributions were made.

In addition to s.342A, it is still open to the trustee in bankruptcy to bring a claim pursuant to IA 1986, ss.339 to 342 if there is evidence of the following:

(a)   where there has been a transaction at an undervalue during the past five years ending with the day of the presentation of the bankruptcy petition; or

(b)   within the period of two years ending with the day of the presentation of the bankruptcy petition, the individual intends to and seeks to put his/her spouse in a better position than they would have been in upon the incidence of his/her bankruptcy. Where there is a subjective desire to prefer then there may be a preference pursuant to IA 1986, s.340. Where the court holds that there has been a preference on a transaction at an undervalue it has extensive powers under s.342 to rectify the position to what it would have been had the unlawful transaction not been performed.

The circumstances in which ss.339 and 340 will apply to Pension Sharing Orders may be limited because it will be the court who sanctions the order and not the individual parties. Further, provided the individual's pension contributions are not deemed to be excessive they will be protected by WRPA 1999, s.11.

Sections 339 and 340 may serve as a useful safety net where the trustee in bankruptcy is unable to satisfy the requirements of ss.342A to 342C but believes that prior to his/her bankruptcy the individual entered into an unlawful arrangement with their spouse.

Matrimonial Causes Act 1973

As amended by Domicile and Matrimonial Proceedings Act 1973, s.6, Domestic Proceedings and Magistrates' Courts Act 1978, s.63, Administration of Justice Act 1982, s.51, Matrimonial and Family Proceedings Act 1984, ss.3, 4, 5, Family Law Reform Act 1987, Sched. 2, Education Act 1993, Sched. 19, Pensions Act 1995, s.166, Family Law Act 1996, Sched. 8, Welfare Reform and Pensions Act 1999, Scheds 3, 4, Child Support, Pensions and Social Security Act 2000, Sched. 3 and the Maintenance Orders (Backdating) Order 1993, SI 1993/623.

PART I

Divorce

5. Refusal of decree in five year separation cases on grounds of grave hardship to respondent

(1)   The respondent to a petition for divorce in which the petitioner alleges five years' separation may oppose the grant of a decree on the ground that the dissolution of the marriage will result in grave financial or other hardship to him and that it would in all the circumstances be wrong to dissolve the marriage.

(2)   Where the grant of a decree is opposed by virtue of this section, then –

(a)   if the court finds that the petitioner is entitled to rely in support of this petition on the fact of five years' separation and makes no such finding as to any other fact mentioned in section 1(2) above, and

(b)   if apart from this section the court would grant a decree on the petition,

the court shall consider all the circumstances, including the conduct of the parties to the marriage and the interests of those parties and of any children or other persons concerned, and if of opinion that the dissolution of the marriage will result in grave financial or other hardship to the respondent and that it would in all the circumstances be wrong to dissolve the marriage it shall dismiss the petition.

(3) For the purposes of this section hardship shall include the loss of the chance of acquiring any benefit which the respondent might acquire if the marriage were not dissolved.

10. Proceedings after decree nisi: special protection for respondent in separation cases

(1) Where in any case the court has granted a decree of divorce on the basis of a finding that the petitioner was entitled to rely in support of his petition on the fact of two years' separation coupled with the respondent's consent to a decree being granted and has made no such finding as to any other fact mentioned in section 1(2) above, the court may, on an application made by the respondent at any time before the decree is made absolute, rescind the decree if it is satisfied that the petitioner misled the respondent (whether intentionally or unintentionally) about any matter which the respondent took into account in deciding to give his consent.

(2) The following provisions of this section apply where –

    (a) the respondent to a petition for divorce in which the petitioner alleged two years' or five years' separation coupled, in the former case, with the respondent's consent to a decree being granted, has applied to the court for consideration under subsection (3) below of his financial position after the divorce; and

    (b) the court has granted a decree on the petition on the basis of a finding that the petitioner was entitled to rely in support of his petition on the fact of two years' or five years' separation (as the case may be) and has made no such finding as to any other fact mentioned in section 1(2) above.

(3) The court hearing an application by the respondent under subsection (2) above shall consider all the circumstances, including the age, health, conduct, earning capacity, financial resources and financial obligations of each of the parties, and the financial position of the respondent as, having regard to the divorce, it is likely to be after the death of the petitioner should the petitioner die first; and, subject to subsection (4) below, the court shall not make the decree absolute unless it is satisfied –

    (a) that the petitioner should not be required to make any financial provision for the respondent, or

    (b) that the financial provision made by the petitioner for the respondent is reasonable and fair or the best that can be made in the circumstances.

(4) The court may if it thinks fit makes the decree absolute notwith-standing the requirements of subsection (3) above if –

    (a) it appears that there are circumstances making it desirable that the decree should be made absolute without delay, and

    (b) the court has obtained a satisfactory undertaking from the petitioner that he will make such financial provision for the respondent as the court may approve.

PART II

Financial provision and property adjustment orders

21. Financial provision and property adjustment orders

(1) The financial provision orders for the purposes of this Act are the orders for periodical or lump sum provision available (subject to the provisions of this Act) under section 23 below for the purpose of adjusting the financial position of the parties to a marriage and any children of the family in connection with proceedings for divorce, nullity of marriage or judicial separation and under section 27(6) below on proof of neglect by one party to a marriage to provide, or to make a proper contribution towards, reasonable maintenance for the other or a child of the family, that is to say –

    (a) any order for periodical payments in favour of a party to a marriage under section 23(1)(a) or 27(6)(a) or in favour of a child of the family under section 23(1)(d), (2) or (4) or 27(6)(d);

    (b) any order for secured periodical payments in favour of a party to a marriage under section 23(1)(b) or 27(6)(b) or in favour of a child of the family under section 23(1)(e), (2) or (4) or 27(6)(e); and

    (c) any order for lump sum provision in favour of a party to a marriage under section 23(1)(c) or 27(6)(c) or in favour of a child of the family under section 23(1)(f), (2) or (4) or 27(6)(f);

and references in this Act (except in paragraphs 17(1) and 23 of Schedule 1 below) to periodical payments orders, secured period-ical payments orders, and orders for the payment of a lump sum are references to all or some of the financial provision orders requiring the sort of financial provision in question according as the context of each reference may require.

(2) The property adjustment orders for the purposes of this Act are the orders dealing with property rights available (subject to the provisions of this Act) under section 24 below for the purpose of

adjusting the financial position of the parties to a marriage and any children of the family on or after the grant of a decree of divorce, nullity of marriage or judicial separation, that is to say –

(a) any order under subsection (1)(a) of that section for a transfer of property;

(b) any order under subsection (1)(b) of that section for a settlement of property; and

(c) any order under subsection (1)(c) or (d) of that section for a variation of settlement.

21A. Pension sharing orders

(1) For the purposes of this Act, a pension sharing order is an order which –

(a) provides that one party's –

(i) shareable rights under a specified pension arrangement, or

(ii) shareable state scheme rights,

be subject to pension sharing for the benefit of the other party, and

(b) specifies the percentage value to be transferred.

(2) In subsection (1) above –

(a) the reference to shareable rights under a pension arrange-ment is to rights in relation to which pensions sharing is available under Chapter I of Part IV of the Welfare Reform and Pensions Act 1999, or under corresponding Northern Ireland legislation,

(b) the reference to shareable state scheme rights is to rights in relation to which pensions sharing is available under Chapter II of Part IV of the Welfare Reform and Pensions Act 1999, or under corresponding Northern Ireland legislation, and

(c) 'party' means a party to a marriage.

PART II

Ancillary relief in connection with divorce proceedings, etc.

22. Maintenance pending suit

On a petition for divorce, nullity of marriage or judicial separation, the court may make an order for maintenance pending suit, that is to say, an order requiring either party to the marriage to make to the other such periodical payments for his or her maintenance and for such term, being a term beginning not earlier than the date of the presentation of the petition and ending with the date of the determination of the suit, as the court thinks reasonable.

23. Financial provision orders in connection with divorce proceedings etc.

(1) On granting a decree of divorce, a decree of nullity of marriage or a decree of judicial separation or at any time thereafter (whether, in the case of a decree of divorce or of nullity of marriage, before or after the decree is made absolute), the court may make any one or more of the following orders, that is to say –

(a) an order that either party to the marriage shall make to the other such periodical payments, for such term, as may be specified in the order;

(b) an order that either party to the marriage shall secure to the other to the satisfaction of the court such periodical payments, for such term, as may be so specified;

(c) an order that either party to the marriage shall pay to the other such lump sum or sums as may be so specified;

(d) an order that a party to the marriage shall make to such person as may be specified in the order for the benefit of a child of the family, or to such a child, such periodical payments, for such term, as may be so specified;

(e) an order that a party to the marriage shall secure to such person as may be so specified for the benefit of such a child, or to such a child, to the satisfaction of the court, such periodical payments, for such term, as may be so specified;

(f) an order that a party to the marriage shall pay to such person as may be so specified for the benefit of such a child, or to such a child, such lump sum as may be so specified;

subject, however, in the case of an order under paragraph (d), (e) or (f) above, to the restrictions imposed by section 29(1) and (3) below on the making of financial provision orders in favour of children who have attained the age of eighteen.

(2) The court may also, subject to those restrictions, make any one or more of the orders mentioned in subsection (1)(d), (e) and (f) above –

(a) in any proceedings for divorce, nullity of marriage or judicial separation, before granting a decree; and

(b) where any such proceedings are dismissed after the beginning of the trial, either forthwith or within a reasonable period after the dismissal.

(3) Without prejudice to the generality of subsection (1)(c) or (f) above –

    (a) an order under this section that a party to a marriage shall pay a lump sum to the other party may be made for the purpose of enabling that other party to meet any liabilities or expenses reasonably incurred by him or her in maintaining himself or herself or any child of the family before making an application for an order under this section in his or her favour;

    (b) an order under this section for the payment of a lump sum to or for the benefit of a child of the family may be made for the purpose of enabling any liabilities or expenses reasonably incurred by or for the benefit of that child before the making of an application for an order under this section in his favour to be met; and

    (c) an order under this section for the payment of a lump sum may provide for the payment of that sum by instalments of such amount as may be specified in the order and may require the payment of the instalments to be secured to the satisfaction of the court.

(4) The power of the court under subsection (1) or (2)(a) above to make an order in favour of a child of the family shall be exercisable from time to time; and where the court makes an order in favour of a child under subsection (2)(b) above, it may from time to time, subject to the restrictions mentioned in subsection (1) above, make a further order in his favour of any of the kinds mentioned in subsection (1)(d), (e) or (f) above.

(5) Without prejudice to the power to give a direction under section 30 below for the settlement of an instrument by conveyancing counsel, where an order is made under subsection (1)(a), (b) or (c) above on or after granting a decree of divorce or nullity of marriage, neither the order nor any settlement made in pursuance of the order shall take effect unless the decree has been made absolute.

(6) Where the court –

    (a) makes an order under this section for the payment of a lump sum; and

    (b) directs –

        (i) that payment of that sum or any part of it shall be deferred; or

        (ii) that that sum or any part of it shall be paid by instalments, the court may order that the amount deferred or the instalments shall carry interest at such rate as may be specified by the order from such date, not earlier than the date of the order, as may be so specified, until the date when payment of it is due.

24. Property adjustment orders in connection with divorce proceedings, etc.

(1) On granting a decree of divorce, a decree of nullity of marriage or a decree of judicial separation or at any time thereafter (whether, in the case of a decree of divorce or of nullity of marriage, before or after the decree is made absolute), the court may make any one or more of the following orders, that is to say –

   (a) an order that a party to the marriage shall transfer to the other party, to any child of the family or to such person as may be specified in the order for the benefit of such a child such property as may be so specified, being property to which the first-mentioned party is entitled, either in possession or reversion;

   (b) an order that a settlement of such property as may be so specified, being property to which a party to the marriage is so entitled, be made to the satisfaction of the court for the benefit of the other party to the marriage and of the children of the family or either or any of them;

   (c) an order varying for the benefit of the parties to the marriage and of the children of the family or either or any of them any ante-nuptial or post-nuptial settlement (including such a settlement made by will or codicil) made on the parties to the marriage, other than one in the form of a pension arrangement (within the meaning of section 25D below);

   (d) an order extinguishing or reducing the interest of either of the parties to the marriage under any such settlement, other than one in the form of a pension arrangement (within the meaning of section 25D below);

subject, however, in the case of any order under paragraph (a) above, to the restrictions imposed by section 29(1) and (3) below on the making of orders for a transfer of property in favour of children who have attained the age of eighteen.

(2) The court may make an order under subsection (1)(c) above notwithstanding that there are no children of the family.

(3) Without prejudice to the power to give a direction under section 30 below for the settlement of an instrument by conveyancing counsel, where an order is made under this section on or after granting a decree of divorce or nullity of marriage, neither the

order nor any settlement made in pursuance of the order shall take effect unless the decree has been made absolute.

24A. Orders for sale of property

(1) Where the court makes under section 23 or 24 of this Act a secured periodical payments order, an order for the payment of a lump sum or a property adjustment order, then, on making that order or at any time thereafter, the court may make a further order for the sale of such property as may be specified in the order, being property in which or in the proceeds of sale of which either or both of the parties to the marriage has or have a beneficial interest, either in possession or reversion.

(2) Any order made under subsection (1) above may contain such consequential or supplementary provisions as the court thinks fit and, without prejudice to the generality of the foregoing provision, may include –

(a) provision requiring the making of a payment out of the proceeds of sale of the property to which the order relates, and

(b) provision requiring any such property to be offered for sale to a person, or class of persons, specified in the order.

(3) Where an order is made under subsection (1) above on or after the grant of a decree of divorce or nullity of marriage, the order shall not take effect unless the decree has been made absolute.

(4) Where an order is made under subsection (1) above, the court may direct that the order, or such provision thereof as the court may specify, shall not take effect until the occurrence of an event specified by the court or the expiration of a period so specified.

(5) Where an order under subsection (1) above contains a provision requiring the proceeds of sale of the property to which the order relates to be used to secure periodical payments to a party to the marriage, the order shall cease to have effect on the death or re-marriage of that person.

(6) Where a party to a marriage has a beneficial interest in any property, or in the proceeds of sale thereof, and some other person who is not a party to the marriage also has a beneficial interest in that property or in the proceeds of sale thereof, then, before deciding whether to make an order under this section in relation to that property, it shall be the duty of the court to give that other person an opportunity to make representations with respect to the order; and any representations made by that other person shall be included among the circumstances to which the court is required to have regard under section 25(1) below.

24B. **Pension sharing orders in connection with divorce proceedings etc.**

(1) On granting a decree of divorce or a decree of nullity of marriage or at any time thereafter (whether before or after the decree is made absolute), the court may, on an application made under this section, make one or more pension sharing orders in relation to the marriage.

(2) A pension sharing order under this section is not to take effect unless the decree on or after which it is made has been made absolute.

(3) A pension sharing order under this section may not be made in relation to a pension arrangement which –

    (a) is the subject of a pension sharing order in relation to the marriage, or

    (b) has been the subject of pension sharing between the parties to the marriage.

(4) A pension sharing order under this section may not be made in relation to shareable state scheme rights if –

    (a) such rights are the subject of a pension sharing order in relation to the marriage, or

    (b) such rights have been the subject of pension sharing between the parties to the marriage.

(5) A pension sharing order under this section may not be made in relation to the rights of a person under a pension arrangement if there is in force a requirement imposed by virtue of section 25B or 25C below which relates to benefits or future benefits to which he is entitled under the pension arrangement.

24C. **Pension sharing orders: duty to stay**

(1) No pension sharing order may be made so as to take effect before the end of such period after the making of the order as may be prescribed by regulations made by the Lord Chancellor.

(2) The power to make regulations under this section shall be exercisable by statutory instrument which shall be subject to annulment in pursuance of a resolution of either House of Parliament.

24D. **Pension sharing orders: apportionment of charges**

If a pension sharing order relates to rights under a pension arrangement, the court may include in the order provision about the apportionment between the parties of any charge under section 41 of the Welfare Reform and Pensions Act 1999 (charges in respect of pension sharing costs), or under corresponding Northern Ireland legislation.

25. Matters to which court is to have regard in deciding how to exercise its powers under ss.23, 24 and 24A

(1) It shall be the duty of the court in deciding whether to exercise its powers under section 23, 24, 24A or 24B above and, if so, in what manner, to have regard to all the circumstances of the case, first consideration being given to the welfare while a minor of any child of the family who has not attained the age of eighteen.

(2) As regards the exercise of the powers of the court under section 23(1)(a), (b) or (c), 24, 24A or 24B above in relation to a party to the marriage, the court shall in particular have regard to the following matters –

   (a) the income, earning capacity, property and other financial resources which each of the parties to the marriage has or is likely to have in the foreseeable future, including in the case of earning capacity any increase in that capacity which it would in the opinion of the court be reasonable to expect a party to the marriage to take steps to acquire;

   (b) the financial needs, obligations and responsibilities which each of the parties to the marriage has or is likely to have in the foreseeable future;

   (c) the standard of living enjoyed by the family before the breakdown of the marriage;

   (d) the age of each party to the marriage and the duration of the marriage;

   (e) any physical or mental disability of either of the parties to the marriage;

   (f) the contributions which each of the parties has made or is likely in the foreseeable future to make to the welfare of the family, including any contributions by looking after the home or caring for the family;

   (g) the conduct of each of the parties, if that conduct is such that it would in the opinion of the court be inequitable to disregard it;

   (h) in the case of proceedings for divorce or nullity of marriage, the value to each of the parties to the marriage of any benefit which, by reason of the dissolution or annulment of the marriage, that party will lose the chance of acquiring.

(3) As regards the exercise of the powers of the court under section 23(1)(d), (e) or (f), (2) or (4), 24 or 24A above in relation to a child of the family, the court shall in particular have regard to the following matters –

   (a) the financial needs of the child;

   (b) the income, earning capacity (if any), property and other financial resources of the child;

    (c)   any physical or mental disability of the child;

    (d)   the manner in which he was being and in which the parties to the marriage expected him to be educated or trained;

    (e)   the consideration mentioned in relation to the parties to the marriage in paragraphs (a), (b), (c) and (e) of subsection (2) above.

(4)   As regards the exercise of the powers of the court under section 23(1)(d), (e) or (f), (2) or (4), 24 or 24A above against a party to a marriage in favour of a child of the family who is not the child of that party, the court shall also have regard –

    (a)   to whether the party assumed any responsibility for the child's maintenance, and, if so, to the extent to which, and the basis upon which, that party assumed such responsibility and to the length of time for which that party discharged such responsibility;

    (b)   to whether in assuming and discharging such responsibility that party did so knowing that the child was not his or her own;

    (c)   to the liability of any other person to maintain the child.

25A.   Exercise of court's powers in favour of party to marriage on decree of divorce or nullity of marriage

(1)   Where on or after the grant of a decree of divorce or nullity of marriage the court decides to exercise its powers under section 23(1)(a), (b) or (c), 24, 24A or 24B above in favour of a party to the marriage, it shall be the duty of the court to consider whether it would be appropriate so to exercise those powers that the financial obligations of each party towards the other will be terminated as soon after the grant of the decree as the court considers just and reasonable.

(2)   Where a court decides in such a case to make a periodical payments or secured periodical payments order in favour of a party to the marriage, the court shall in particular consider whether it would be appropriate to require those payments to be made or secured only for such term as would in the opinion of the court be sufficient to enable the party in whose favour the order is made to adjust without undue hardship to the termination of his or her financial dependence on the other party.

(3)   Where on or after the grant of a decree of divorce or nullity of marriage an application is made by a party to the marriage for a periodical payments or secured periodical payments order in his or her favour, then, if the court considers that no continuing obligation should be imposed on either party to make or secure periodical payments in favour of the other, the court may dismiss the

application with a direction that the applicant shall not be entitled to make any further application in relation to that marriage for an order under section 23(1)(a) or (b) above.

25B. Pensions

(1) The matters to which the court is to have regard under section 25(2) above include –

   (a) in the case of paragraph (a), any benefits under a pension arrangement which a party to the marriage has or is likely to have, and

   (b) in the case of paragraph (h), any benefits under a pension arrangement which, by reason of the dissolution or annulment of the marriage, a party to the marriage will lose the chance of acquiring,

   and, accordingly, in relation to benefits under a pension arrangement, section 25(2)(a) above shall have effect as if 'in the foreseeable future' were omitted.

(2) *repealed*

(3) The following provisions apply where, having regard to any benefits under a pension arrangement, the court determines to make an order under section 23 above.

(4) To the extent to which the order is made having regard to any benefits under a pension arrangement, the order may require the person responsible for the pension arrangement in question, if at any time any payment in respect of any benefits under the arrangement becomes due to the party with pension rights, to make a payment for the benefit of the other party.

(5) The order must express the amount of any payment required to be made by virtue of subsection (4) above as a percentage of the payment which becomes due to the party with pension rights.

(6) Any such payment by the person responsible for the arrangement –

   (a) shall discharge so much of his liability to the party with pension rights as corresponds to the amount of the payment, and

   (b) shall be treated for all purposes as a payment made by the party with pension rights in or towards the discharge of his liability under the order.

(7) Where the party with pension rights has a right of commutation under the arrangement, the order may require him to exercise it to any extent; and this section applies to any payment due in consequence of commutation in pursuance of the order as it applies to other payments in respect of benefits under the arrangement.

(7A) The power conferred by subsection (7) above may not be exercised for the purpose of commuting a benefit payable to the party with pension rights to a benefit payable to the other party.

(7B) The power conferred by subsection (4) or (7) above may not be exercised in relation to a pension arrangement which –

(a) is the subject of a pension sharing order in relation to the marriage, or

(b) has been the subject of pension sharing between the parties to the marriage.

(7C) In subsection (1) above, references to benefits under a pension arrangement include any benefits by way of pension, whether under a pension arrangement or not.

25C. Pensions: lump sums

(1) The power of the court under section 23 above to order a party to a marriage to pay a lump sum to the other party includes, where the benefits which the party with pension rights has or is likely to have under a pension arrangement include any lump sum payable in respect of his death, power to make any of the following provision by the order.

(2) The court may –

(a) if the person responsible for the pension arrangement in question has power to determine the person to whom the sum, or any part of it, is to be paid, require him to pay the whole or part of that sum, when it becomes due, to the other party,

(b) if the party with pension rights has power to nominate the person to whom the sum, or any part of it, is to be paid, require the party with pension rights to nominate the other party in respect of the whole or part of that sum,

(c) in any other case, require the person responsible for the pension arrangement in question to pay the whole or part of that sum, when it becomes due, for the benefit of the other party instead of to the person to whom, apart from the order, it would be paid.

(3) Any payment by the person responsible for the arrangement under an order made under section 23 above by virtue of this section shall discharge so much of his liability in respect of the party with pension rights as corresponds to the amount of the payment.

(4) The powers conferred by this section may not be exercised in relation to a pension arrangement which –

(a) is the subject of a pension sharing order in relation to the marriage, or

(b) has been the subject of pension sharing between the parties to the marriage.

25D. Pensions: supplementary

(1) Where –

(a) an order made under section 23 above by virtue of section 25B or 25C above imposes any requirement on the person responsible for a pension arrangement ('the first arrangement') and the party with pension rights acquires rights under another pension arrangement ('the new arrangement') which are derived (directly or indirectly) from the whole of his rights under the first arrangement, and

(b) the person responsible for the new arrangement has been given notice in accordance with regulations made by the Lord Chancellor,

the order shall have effect as if it had been made instead in respect of the person responsible for the new arrangement.

(2) The Lord Chancellor may by regulations –

(a) in relation to any provision of sections 25B or 25C above which authorises the court making an order under section 23 above to require the person responsible for a pension arrangement to make a payment for the benefit of the other party, make provisions as to the person to whom, and the terms on which, the payment is to be made,

(ab) make, in relation to payment under a mistaken belief as to the continuation in force of a provision included by virtue of section 25B or 25C above in an order under section 23 above, provision about the rights or liabilities of the payer, the payee or the person to whom the payment was due,

(b) require notices to be given in respect of changes of circumstances relevant to such orders which include provision made by virtue of sections 25B and 25C above,

(ba) make provision for the person responsible for a pension arrangement to be discharged in prescribed circumstances from a requirement imposed by virtue of section 25B or 25C above,

(c) *repealed*

(d) *repealed*

(e) make provision about calculation and verification in relation to the valuation of –

(i)   benefits under a pension arrangement, or

(ii)   shareable state scheme rights,

for the purposes of the court's functions in connection with the exercise of any of its powers under this Part of this Act.

(2A) Regulations under subsection (2)(e) above may include –

(a)   provision for calculation or verification in accordance with guidance from time to time prepared by a prescribed person, and

(b)   provision by reference to regulations under section 30 or 49(4) of the Welfare Reform and Pensions Act 1999.

(2B) Regulations under subsection (2) above may make different provision for different cases.

(2C) Power to make regulations under this section shall be exercisable by statutory instrument which shall be subject to annulment in pursuance of a resolution of either House of Parliament.

(3)   In this section and sections 25B and 25C above –

'occupational pension scheme' has the same meaning as in the Pension Schemes Act 1993;

'the party with pension rights' means the party to the marriage who has or is likely to have benefits under a pension arrangement and 'the other party' means the other party to the marriage;

'pension arrangement' means –

(a)   an occupational pension scheme,

(b)   a personal pension scheme,

(c)   a retirement annuity contract,

(d)   an annuity or insurance policy purchased, or transferred, for the purpose of giving effect to rights under an occupational pension scheme or a personal pension scheme, and

(e)   an annuity purchased, or entered into, for the purpose of discharging liability in respect of a pension credit under section 29(1)(b) of the Welfare Reform and Pensions Act 1999 or under corresponding Northern Ireland legislation;

'personal pension scheme' has the same meaning as in the Pension Schemes Act 1993;

'prescribed' means prescribed by regulations;

'retirement annuity contract' means a contract or scheme approved under Chapter III of Part XIV of the Income and Corporation Taxes Act 1988;

'shareable state scheme rights' has the same meaning as in section 21A(1) above; and

'trustees or managers', in relation to an occupational pension scheme or a personal pension scheme, means –

    (a)   in the case of a scheme established under a trust, the trustees of the scheme, and

    (b)   in any other case, the managers of the scheme.

(4)   In this section and sections 25B and 25C above, references to the person responsible for a pension arrangement are –

    (a)   in the case of an occupational pension scheme or a personal pension scheme, to the trustees or managers of the scheme,

    (b)   in the case of a retirement annuity contract or an annuity falling within paragraph (d) or (e) of the definition of 'pension arrangement' above, the provider of the annuity, and

    (c)   in the case of an insurance policy falling within paragraph (d) of the definition of that expression, the insurer.

26.   Commencement of proceedings for ancillary relief, etc.

(1)   Where a petition for divorce, nullity of marriage or judicial separation has been presented, then, subject to subsection (2) below, proceedings for maintenance pending suit under section 22 above, for a financial provision order under section 23 above, or for a property adjustment order may be begun, subject to and in accordance with rules of court, at any time after the presentation of the petition.

(2)   Rules of court may provide, in such cases as may be prescribed by the rules –

    (a)   that applications for any such relief as is mentioned in subsection (1) above shall be made in the petition or answer; and

    (b)   that applications for any such relief which are not so made, or are not made until after the expiration of such period following the presentation of the petition or filing of the answer as may be so prescribed, shall be made only with the leave of the court.

PART II

Financial provision in case of neglect to maintain

27. Financial provision orders, etc., in case of neglect by party to marriage to maintain other party or child of the family

(1) Either party to a marriage may apply to the court for an order under this section on the ground that the other party to the marriage (in this section referred to as the respondent) –

(a) has failed to provide reasonable maintenance for the applicant, or

(b) has failed to provide, or to make a proper contribution towards, reasonable maintenance for any child of the family.

(2) The court shall not entertain an application under this section unless –

(a) the applicant or the respondent is domiciled in England and Wales on the date of the application; or

(b) the applicant has been habitually resident there throughout the period of one year ending with that date; or

(c) the respondent is resident there on that date.

(3) Where an application under this section is made on the ground mentioned in subsection (1)(a) above, then, in deciding –

(a) whether the respondent has failed to provide reasonable maintenance for the applicant, and

(b) what order, if any, to make under this section in favour of the applicant,

the court shall have regard to all the circumstances of the case including the matters mentioned in section 25(2) above, and where an application is also made under this section in respect of a child of the family who has not attained the age of eighteen, first consideration shall be given to the welfare of the child while a minor.

(3A) Where an application under this section is made on the ground mentioned in subsection (1)(b) above then, in deciding –

(a) whether the respondent has failed to provide, or to make a proper contribution towards, reasonable maintenance for the child of the family to whom the application relates, and

(b) what order, if any, to make under this section in favour of the child,

the court shall have regard to all the circumstances of the case including the matters mentioned in section 25(3)(a) to (e) above, and where the child of the family to whom the application relates is not the child of the respondent, including also the matters mentioned in section 25(4) above.

(3B) In relation to an application under this section on the ground mentioned in subsection (1)(a) above, section 25(2)(c) above shall have effect as if for the reference therein to the breakdown of the marriage there were substituted a reference to the failure to provide reasonable maintenance for the applicant, and in relation to an application under this section on the ground mentioned in subsection (1)(b) above, section 25(2)(c) above (as it applies by virtue of section 25(3)(e) above) shall have effect as if for the reference therein to the breakdown of the marriage there were substituted a reference to the failure to provide, or to make a proper contribution towards, reasonable maintenance for the child of the family to whom the application relates.

(4) *repealed*

(5) Where on an application under this section it appears to the court that the applicant or any child of the family to whom the application relates is in immediate need of financial assistance, but it is not yet possible to determine what order, if any, should be made on the application, the court may make an interim order for maintenance, that is to say, an order requiring the respondent to make to the applicant until the determination of the application such periodical payments as the court thinks reasonable.

(6) Where on an application under this section the applicant satisfies the court of any ground mentioned in subsection (1) above, the court may make any one or more of the following orders –

   (a) an order that the respondent shall make to the applicant such periodical payments, for such term, as may be specified in the order;

   (b) an order that the respondent shall secure to the applicant, to the satisfaction of the court, such periodical payments, for such term, as may be so specified;

   (c) an order that the respondent shall pay to the applicant such lump sum as may be so specified;

   (d) an order that the respondent shall make to such person as may be specified in the order for the benefit of the child to whom the application relates, or to that child, such periodical payments, for such term, as may be so specified;

   (e) an order that the respondent shall secure to such person as may be so specified for the benefit of that child, or to that child, to the satisfaction of the court, such periodical payments, for such term, as may be so specified;

(f) an order that the respondent shall pay to such person as may be so specified for the benefit of that child, or to that child, such lump sum as may be so specified;

subject, however, in the case of an order under paragraph (d), (e) or (f) above, to the restrictions imposed by section 29(1) and (3) below on the making of financial provision orders in favour of children who have attained the age of eighteen.

(6A) An application for the variation under section 31 of this Act of a periodical payments order or secured periodical payments order made under this section in favour of a child may, if the child has attained the age of sixteen, be made by the child himself.

(6B) Where a periodical payments order made in favour of a child under this section ceases to have effect on the date on which the child attains the age of sixteen or at any time after that date but before or on the date on which he attains the age of eighteen, then if, on an application made to the court for an order under this subsection, it appears to the court that –

(a) the child is, will be or (if an order were made under this subsection) would be receiving instruction at an education establishment or undergoing training for a trade, profession or vocation, whether or not he also is, will be or would be in gainful employment; or

(b) there are special circumstances which justify the making of an order under this subsection,

the court shall have power by order to revive the first mentioned order from such date as the court may specify, not being earlier than the date of the making of the application, and to exercise its power under section 31 of this Act in relation to any order so revived.

(7) Without prejudice to the generality of subsection (6)(c) or (f) above, an order under this section for the payment of a lump sum –

(a) may be made for the purpose of enabling any liabilities or expenses reasonably incurred in maintaining the applicant or any child of the family to whom the application relates before the making of the application to be met;

(b) may provide for the payment of that sum by instalments of such amount as may be specified in the order and may require the payment of the instalments to be secured to the satisfaction of the court.

(8) *repealed*

PART II

Additional provisions with respect to financial provision and property adjustment orders

28. Duration of continuing financial provision orders in favour of party to marriage, and effect of remarriage

(1) Subject in the case of an order made on or after the grant of a decree of divorce or nullity of marriage to the provisions of sections 25A(2) above and 31(7) below, the term to be specified in a periodical payments or secured periodical payments order in favour of a party to a marriage shall be such term as the court thinks fit, except that the term shall not begin before or extend beyond the following limits, that is to say –

(a) in the case of a periodical payments order, the term shall begin not earlier than the date of the making of an application for the order, and shall be so defined as not to extend beyond the death of either of the parties to the marriage or, where the order is made on or after the grant of a decree of divorce or nullity of marriage, the remarriage of the party in whose favour the order is made; and

(b) in the case of a secured periodical payments orders, the term shall begin not earlier than the date of the making of an application for the order, and shall be so defined as not to extend beyond the death or, where the order is made on or after the grant of such a decree, the remarriage of the party in whose favour the order is made.

(1A) Where a periodical payments or secured periodical payments order in favour of a party to a marriage is made on or after the grant of a decree of divorce or nullity of marriage, the court may direct that that party shall not be entitled to apply under section 31 below for the extension of the term specified in the order.

(2) Where a periodical payments or secured periodical payments order in favour of a party to a marriage is made otherwise than on or after the grant of a decree of divorce or nullity of marriage, and the marriage in question is subsequently dissolved or annulled but the order continues in force, the order shall, notwithstanding anything in it, cease to have effect on the remarriage of that party, except in relation to any arrears due under it on the date of the remarriage.

(3) If after the grant of a decree dissolving or annulling a marriage either party to that marriage remarries whether at any time before or after the commencement of this Act, that party shall not be entitled to apply, by reference to the grant of that decree, for a

financial provision order in his or her favour, or for a property adjustment order, against the other party to that marriage.

29. Duration of continuing financial provision orders in favour of children, and age limit on making certain orders in their favour

(1) Subject to subsection (3) below, no financial provision order and no order for a transfer of property under section 24(1)(a) above shall be made in favour of a child who has attained the age of eighteen.

(2) The term to be specified in a periodical payments or secured periodical payments order in favour of a child may begin with the date of the making of an application for the order in question or any later date or a date ascertained in accordance with subsection (5) or (6) below but –

(a) shall not in the first instance extend beyond the date of the birthday of the child next following his attaining the upper limit of the compulsory school age (construed in accordance with section 277 of the Education Act 1993) unless the court considers that in the circumstances of the case the welfare of the child requires that it should extend to a later date; and

(b) shall not in any event, subject to subsection (3) below, extend beyond the date of the child's eighteenth birthday.

(3) Subsection (1) above, and paragraph (b) of subsection (2), shall not apply in the case of a child, if it appears to the court that –

(a) the child is, or will be, or if an order were made without complying with either or both of those provisions would be, receiving instruction at an educational establishment or under-going training for a trade, professions or vocation, whether or not he is also, or will also be, in gainful employment; or

(b) there are special circumstances which justify the making of an order without complying with either or both of those provisions.

(4) Any periodical payments order in favour of a child shall, notwithstanding anything in the order, cease to have effect on the death of the person liable to make payments under the order, except in relation to any arrears due under the order on the date of the death.

(5) Where –

(a) a maintenance calculation ('the current calculation') is in force with respect to a child; and

      (b)   an application is made under Part II of this Act for a periodical payments or secured periodical payments order in favour of that child –

           (i)   in accordance with section 8 of the Child Support Act 1991, and

           (ii) before the end of the period of 6 months beginning with the making of the current calculation

the term to be specified in any such order made on that application may be expressed to begin on, or at any time after, the earliest permitted date.

(6)   For the purposes of subsection (5) above, 'the earliest permitted date' is whichever is the later of –

      (a)   the date 6 months before the application is made; or

      (b)   the date on which the current calculation took effect or, where successive maintenance calculations have been continuously in force with respect to a child, on which the first of those calculations took effect.

(7)   Where –

      (a)   a maintenance calculation ceases to have effect by or under any provision of the Child Support Act 1991; and

      (b)   an application is made, before the end of the period of 6 months beginning with the relevant date, for a periodical payments or secured periodical payments order in favour of a child with respect to whom that maintenance calculation was in force immediately before it ceased to have effect,

the term to be specified in any such order made on that application may begin with the date on which that maintenance calculation ceased to have effect.

(8)   In this subsection (7)(b) above –

      (a)   where the maintenance calculation ceased to have effect, the relevant date is the date on which it so ceased.

      (b)   *repealed*

30. Direction for settlement of instrument for securing payments or effecting property adjustment

Where the court decides to make a financial provision order requiring any payments to be secured or a property adjustment order –

      (a)   it may direct that the matter be referred to one of the conveyancing counsel of the court for him to settle a proper instrument to be executed by all necessary parties; and

(b) where the order is to be made in proceedings for divorce, nullity of marriage or judicial separation it may, if it thinks fit, defer the grant of the decree in question until the instrument has been duly executed.

PART II

Variation, discharge and enforcement of certain orders, etc.

31. Variation, discharge, etc., of certain orders for financial relief

(1) Where the court has made an order to which this section applies, then, subject to the provisions of this section and of section 28(1A) above, the court shall have power to vary or discharge the order or to suspend any provision thereof temporarily and to revive the operation of any provision so suspended.

(2) This section applies to the following orders, that is to say –

(a) any order for maintenance pending suit and any interim order for maintenance;

(b) any periodical payments order;

(c) any secured periodical payments order;

(d) any order made by virtue of section 23(3)(c) or 27(7)(b) above (provision for payment of a lump sum by instalments);

(dd) any deferred order made by virtue of section 23(1)(c) (lump sums) which includes provision made by virtue of –

(i) section 25B(4), or

(ii) section 25C (provision in respect of pension rights);

(e) any order for a settlement of property under section 24(1)(b) or for a variation of settlement under section 24(1)(c) or (d) above, being an order made on or after the grant of a decree of judicial separation;

(f) any order made under section 24A(1) above for the sale of property;

(g) a pension sharing order under section 24B above which is made at a time before the decree has been made absolute.

(2A) Where the court has made an order referred to in subsection 2(a), (b) or (c) above, then, subject to the provisions of this section, the court shall have the power to remit the payment of any arrears due under the order or of any part thereof.

(2B) Where the court has made an order referred to in subsection (2)(dd)(ii) above, this section shall cease to apply to the order on the death of either of the parties to the marriage.

(3) The powers exercisable by the court under this section in relation to an order shall be exercisable also in relation to any instrument executed in pursuance of the order.

(4) The court shall not exercise the powers conferred by this section in relation to an order for a settlement under section 24(1)(b) or for a variation of settlement under section 24(1)(c) or (d) above except on an application made in proceedings –

    (a) for the rescission of the decree of judicial separation by reference to which the order was made, or

    (b) for the dissolution of the marriage in question.

(4A) In relation to an order which falls within paragraph (g) of subsection (2) above ('the subsection (2) order') –

    (a) the powers conferred by this section may be exercised –

        (i) only on an application made before the subsection (2) order has or, but for paragraph (b) below, would have taken effect; and

        (ii) only if, at the time when the application is made, the decree has not been made absolute; and

    (b) an application made in accordance with paragraph (a) above prevents the subsection (2) order from taking effect before the application has been dealt with.

(4B) No variation of a pensions sharing order shall be made so as to take effect before the decree is made absolute.

(4C) The variation of a pension sharing order prevents the order taking effect before the end of such period after the making of the variation as may be prescribed by regulations made by the Lord Chancellor.

(5) Subject to subsections (7A) to (7G) below and without prejudice to any power exercisable by virtue of subsection (2)(d), (dd), (e) or (g) above or otherwise than by virtue of this section. No property adjustment order shall be made on an application for the variation of a periodical payments or secured periodical payments order made (whether in favour of a party to a marriage or in favour of a child of the family) under section 23 above, and no order for the payment of a lump sum shall be made on an application for the variation of a periodical payments or secured periodical payments order in favour of a party to a marriage (whether made under section 23 or under section 27 above).

(6) Where the person liable to make payments under a secured periodical payments order has died, an application under this section relating to that order (and to any order made under section 24A(1) above which requires the proceeds of sale of property to be used

for securing those payments) may be made by the person entitled to payments under the periodical payments order, or by the personal representatives of the deceased person, but no such application shall, except with the permission of the court, be made after the end of the period of six months from the date on which representation in regard to the estate of that person is first taken out.

(7) In exercising the powers conferred by this section the court shall have regard to all the circumstances of the case, first consideration being given to the welfare while a minor of any child of the family who has not attained the age of eighteen, and the circumstances of the case shall include any change in any of the matters to which the court was required to have regard when making the order to which the application relates, and –

(a) in the case of a periodical payments or secured periodical payments order made on or after the grant of a decree of divorce or nullity of marriage, the court shall consider whether in all the circumstances and after having regard to any such change it would be appropriate to vary the order so that payments under the order are required to be made or secured only for such further period as will in the opinion of the court be sufficient (in the light of any proposed exercise by the court, where the marriage has been dissolved, of its powers under subsection (7B) below) to enable the party in whose favour the order was made to adjust without undue hardship to the termination of those payments;

(b) in a case where the party against whom the order was made has died, the circumstances of the case shall also include the changed circumstances resulting from his or her death.

(7A) Subsection (7B) below applies where, after the dissolution of a marriage, the court –

(a) discharges a periodical payments order or secured periodical payments order made in favour of a party to the marriage or

(b) varies such an order so that payments under the order are required to be made or secured only for such further period as is determined by the court.

(7B) The court has power, in addition to any power it has apart from this subsection, to make supplemental provision consisting of any of –

(a) an order for the payment of a lump sum in favour of a party to the marriage

(b) one or more property adjustment orders in favour of a party to the marriage (ba) one or more pension sharing orders;

(c) a direction that the party in whose favour the original order discharged or varied was made is not entitled to make any further application for –

(i) a periodical payments or secured periodical payments order, or

(ii) an extension of the period to which the original order is limited by any variation made by the court.

(7C) An order for the payment of a lump sum made under subsection (7B) above may –

(a) provide for the payment of that sum by instalments of such amount as may be specified in the order and

(b) require the payment of the instalments to be secured to the satisfaction of the court.

(7D) Subsections (7) and (8) of section 22A above apply where the court makes an order for the payment of a lump sum under subsection (7B) above as they apply where it makes such an order under section 22A above.

(7E) If under subsection (7B) above the court makes more than one property adjustment order in favour of the same party to the marriage, each of those orders must fall within a different paragraph of section 21(2) above.

(7F) Sections 24A and 30 above apply where the court makes a property adjustment order under subsection (7B) above as they apply where it makes such an order under section 23A above.

(7G) Subsections (3) to (5) of section 24B above apply in relation to a pension sharing order under subsection (7B) above as they apply in relation to a pension sharing order under that section.

(8) The personal representatives of a deceased person against whom a secured periodical payments order was made shall not be liable for having distributed any part of the estate of the deceased after the expiration of the period of six months referred to in subsection (6) above on the ground that they ought to have taken into account the possibility that the court might permit an application under this section to be made after that period by the person entitled to payments under the order; but this subsection shall not prejudice any power to recover any part of the estate so distributed arising by virtue of the making of an order in pursuance of this section.

(9) In considering for the purposes of subsection (6) above the question when representation was first taken out, a grant limited to settled land or to trust property shall be left out of account and a grant limited to real estate or to personal estate shall be left out of

account unless a grant limited to the remainder of the estate has previously been made or is made at the same time.

(10) Where the court, in exercise of its power, under this section, decides to vary or discharge a periodical payments or secured periodical payments order, then, subject to section 28(1) and (2) above, the court shall have power to direct that the variation or discharge shall not take effect until the expiration of such period as may be specified in the order.

(11) Where –

    (a)   a periodical payments or secured periodical payments order in favour of more than one child ('the order') is in force;

    (b)   the order requires payments specified in it to be made to or for the benefit of more than one child without apportioning those payments between them;

    (c)   a maintenance calculation ('the calculation') is made with respect to one or more, but not all, of the children with respect to whom those payments are to be made; and

    (d)   an application is made, before the end of the period of 6 months beginning with the date on which the calculation was made, for the variation or discharge of the order, the court may, in exercise of its powers under this section to vary or discharge the order, direct that the variation or discharge shall take effect from the date on which the calculation took effect or any later date.

(12) Where –

    (a)   an order ('the child order') of a kind prescribed for the purposes of section 10(1) of the Child Support Act 1991 is affected by a maintenance calculation;

    (b)   on the date on which the child order became so affected there was in force a periodical payments or secured periodical payments order ('the spousal order') in favour of a party to a marriage having the care of the child in whose favour the child order was made; and

    (c)   an application is made, before the end of the period of 6 months beginning with the date on which the maintenance calculation was made, for the spousal order to be varied or discharged,

the court may, in exercise of its powers under this section to vary or discharge the spousal order, direct that the variation or discharge shall take effect from the date on which the child order became so affected or any later date.

(13) For the purposes of subsection (12) above, an order is affected if it ceases to have effect or is modified by or under section 10 of the Child Support Act 1991.

(14) Subsections (11) and (12) above are without prejudice to any other power of the court to direct that the variation of discharge of an order under this section shall take effect from a date earlier than that on which the order for variation or discharge was made.

(15) The power to make regulations under subsection (4C) above shall be exercisable by statutory instrument which shall be subject to annulment in pursuance of a resolution of either House of Parliament.

PART II

Miscellaneous and supplemental

37. Avoidance of transactions intended to prevent or reduce financial relief

(1) For the purposes of this section 'financial relief' means relief under any of the provisions of sections 22, 23, 24, 24B, 27, 31 (except subsection (6)) and 35 above, and any reference in this section to defeating a person's claim for financial relief is a reference to preventing financial relief from being granted to that person, or to that person for the benefit of a child of the family, or reducing the amount of any financial relief which might be so granted, or frustrating or impeding the enforcement of any order which might be or has been made at his instance under any of these provisions.

(2) Where proceedings for financial relief are brought by one person against another, the court may, on the application of the first-mentioned person –

    (a) if it is satisfied that the other party to the proceedings is, with the intention of defeating the claim for financial relief, about to make any disposition or to transfer out of the jurisdiction or otherwise deal with any property, make such order as it thinks fit for restraining the other party from so doing or otherwise for protecting the claim;

    (b) if it is satisfied that the other party has, with that intention, made a reviewable disposition and that if the disposition were set aside financial relief or different financial relief would be granted to the applicant, make an order setting aside the disposition;

    (c) if it is satisfied, in a case where an order has been obtained under any of the provisions mentioned in subsection (1) above by the applicant against the other party, that the other party has, with that intention, made a reviewable disposition, make an order setting aside the disposition;

and an application for the purposes of paragraph (b) above shall be made in the proceedings for the financial relief in question.

(3) Where the court makes an order under subsection (2)(b) or (c) above setting aside a disposition it shall give such consequential directions as it thinks fit for giving effect to the order (including directions requiring the making of any payments or the disposal of any property).

(4) Any disposition made by the other party to the proceedings for financial relief in question (whether before or after the commencement of those proceedings) is a reviewable disposition for the purposes of subsection (2)(b) and (c) above unless it was made for valuable consideration (other than marriage) to a person who, at the time of the disposition, acted in relation to it in good faith and without notice of any intention on the part of the other party to defeat the applicant's claim for financial relief.

(5) Where an application is made under this section with respect to a disposition which took place less than three years before the date of the application or with respect to a disposition or other dealing with property which is about to take place and the court is satisfied –

(a) in a case falling within subsection (2)(a) or (b) above, that the disposition or other dealing would (apart from this section) have the consequence, or

(b) in a case falling within subsection (2)(c) above, that the disposition has had the consequence,

of defeating the applicant's claim for financial relief, it shall be presumed, unless the contrary is shown, that the person who disposed of or is about to dispose of or deal with the property did so or, as the case may be, is about to do so, with the intention of defeating the applicant's claim for financial relief.

(6) In this section 'disposition' does not include any provision contained in a will or codicil but, with that exception, includes any conveyance, assurance or gift of property of any description, whether made by an instrument or otherwise.

(7) This section does not apply to a disposition made before 1st January 1968.

Matrimonial and Family Proceedings Act 1984

As amended by Family Law Act 1996, Sched. 8, Welfare Reform and Pensions Act 1999, s.22, Sched. 12 and the Civil Jurisdiction and Judgments Order 2001, SI 2001/3929.

PART III FINANCIAL RELIEF IN ENGLAND AND WALES AFTER OVERSEAS DIVORCE ETC.

Applications for financial relief

12. **Applications for financial relief after overseas divorce etc.**

(1) Where –

   (a) a marriage has been dissolved or annulled, or the parties to a marriage have been legally separated, by means of judicial or other proceedings in an overseas country, and

   (b) the divorce, annulment or legal separation is entitled to be recognised as valid in England and Wales,

either party to the marriage may apply to the court in the manner prescribed by rules of court for an order for financial relief under this Part of this Act.

(2) If after a marriage has been dissolved or annulled in an overseas country one of the parties to the marriage remarries that party shall not be entitled to make an application in relation to that marriage.

(3) For the avoidance of doubt it is hereby declared that the reference in subsection (2) above to remarriage includes a reference to a marriage which is by law void or voidable.

(4) In this Part of this Act except sections 19, 23, and 24 'order for financial relief' means an order under section 17 or 22 below of a description referred to in that section.

13. Leave of the court required for applications for financial relief

(1) No application for an order for financial relief shall be made under this Part of this Act unless the leave of the court has been obtained in accordance with rules of court; and the court shall not grant leave unless it considers that there is substantial ground for the making of an application for such an order.

(2) The court may grant leave under this section notwithstanding that an order has been made by a court in a country outside England and Wales requiring the other party to the marriage to make any payment or transfer any property to the applicant or a child of the family.

(3) Leave under this section may be granted subject to such conditions as the court thinks fit.

14. Interim orders for maintenance

(1) Where leave is granted under section 13 above for the making of an application for an order for financial relief and it appears to the court that the applicant or any child of the family is in immediate need of financial assistance, the court may make an interim order for maintenance, that is to say, an order requiring the other party to the marriage to make to the applicant or to the child such periodical payments, and for such term, being a term beginning not earlier than the date of the grant of leave and ending with the date of the determination of the application for an order for financial relief, as the court thinks reasonable.

(2) If it appears to the court that the court has jurisdiction to entertain the application for an order for financial relief by reason only of paragraph (c) of section 15(1) below the court shall not make an interim order under this section.

(3) An interim order under subsection (1) above may be made subject to such conditions as the court thinks fit.

15. Jurisdiction of the court

(1) Subject to subsection (2) below, the court shall have jurisdiction to entertain an application for an order for financial relief if any of the following jurisdictional requirements are satisfied, that is to say –

(a) either of the parties to the marriage was domiciled in England and Wales on the date of the application for leave under section 13 above or was so domiciled on the date on which the divorce, annulment or legal separation obtained in the overseas country took effect in that country; or

(b) either of the parties to the marriage was habitually resident in England and Wales throughout the period of one year ending with the date of the application for leave or was so resident throughout the period of one year ending with the date on which the divorce, annulment or legal separation obtained in the overseas country took effect in that country; or

(c) either or both of the parties to the marriage had at the date of the application for leave a beneficial interest in possession in a dwelling-house situated in England or Wales which was at some time during the marriage a matrimonial home of the parties to the marriage.

(2) Where the jurisdiction of the court to entertain proceedings under this Part of this Act would fall to be determined by reference to the jurisdictional requirements imposed by virtue of Part I of the Civil Jurisdiction and Judgments Act 1982 (implementation of certain European conventions) or by virtue of Council Regulation (EC) No. 44/2001 of 22nd December 2000 on jurisdiction and the recognition and enforcement of judgments in civil and commercial matters or then –

(a) satisfaction of the requirements of subsection (1) above shall not obviate the need to satisfy the requirements imposed by virtue of that Regulation or Part I of that Act; and

(b) satisfaction of the requirements imposed by virtue of that Regulation or Part I of that Act shall obviate the need to satisfy the requirements of subsection (1) above;

and the court shall entertain or not entertain the proceedings accordingly.

16. Duty of the court to consider whether England and Wales is appropriate venue for application

(1) Before making an order for financial relief the court shall consider whether in all the circumstances of the case it would be appropriate for such an order to be made by a court in England and Wales, and if the court is not satisfied that it would be appropriate, the court shall dismiss the application.

(2) The court shall in particular have regard to the following matters –

(a) the connection which the parties to the marriage have with England and Wales;

(b) the connection which those parties have with the country in which the marriage was dissolved or annulled or in which they were legally separated;

(c) the connection which those parties have with any other country outside England and Wales;

(d) any financial benefit which the applicant or a child of the family has received, or is likely to receive, in consequence of the divorce, annulment or legal separation, by virtue of any agreement or the operation of the law of a country outside England and Wales;

(e) in a case where an order has been made by a court in a country outside England and Wales requiring the other party to the marriage to make any payment or transfer any property for the benefit of the applicant or a child of the family, the financial relief given by the order and the extent to which the order has been complied with or is likely to be complied with;

(f) any right which the applicant has, or had had, to apply for financial relief from the other party to the marriage under the law of any country outside England and Wales and if the applicant has omitted to exercise that right the reason for that omission;

(g) the availability in England and Wales of any property in respect of which an order under this Part of this Act in favour of the applicant could be made;

(h) the extent to which any order made under this Part of this Act is likely to be enforceable;

(i) the length of time which has elapsed since the date of the divorce, annulment or legal separation.

Orders for financial provision and property adjustment

17. Orders for financial provision and property adjustment

(1) Subject to section 20 below, on an application by a party to a marriage for an order for financial relief under this section, the court may –

(a) make any one or more of the orders which it could make under Part II of the 1973 Act if a decree of divorce, a decree of nullity of marriage or a decree of judicial separation in respect of the marriage had been granted in England and Wales, that is to say –

(i) any order mentioned in section 23(1) of the 1973 Act (financial provision orders); and

(ii) any order mentioned in section 2(1) of that Act (property adjustment orders); and

(b) if the marriage has been dissolved or annulled, make one or more orders each of which would, within the meaning of that Part of that Act, be a pension sharing order in relation to the marriage.

(2) Subject to section 20 below, where the court makes a secured periodical payments order, an order for the payment of a lump sum or a property adjustment order under subsection (1) above, then, on making that order or at any time thereafter, the court may make any order mentioned in section 24A(1) of the 1973 Act (orders for sale of property) which the court would have power to make if the order under subsection (1) above had been made under Part II of the 1973 Act.

18. Matters to which the court is to have regard in exercising its powers under s.17

(1) In deciding whether to exercise its powers under section 17 above and, if so, in what manner the court shall act in accordance with this section.

(2) The court shall have regard to all the circumstances of the case, first consideration being given to the welfare while a minor of any child of the family who has not attained the age of eighteen.

(3) As regards the exercise of those powers in relation to a party to the marriage, the court shall in particular have regard to the matters mentioned in section 25(2)(a) to (h) of the 1973 Act and shall be under duties corresponding with those imposed by section 25A(1) and (2) of the 1973 Act where it decides to exercise under section 17 above powers corresponding with the powers referred to in those subsections.

(3A) The matters to which the court is to have regard under subsection (3) above –

(a) so far as relating to paragraph (a) of section 25(2) of the 1973 Act, include any benefits under a pension arrangement which a party to the marriage has or is likely to have (whether or not in the foreseeable future), and

(b) so far as relating to paragraph (h) of that provision, include any benefits under a pension arrangement which, by reason of the dissolution or annulment of the marriage, a party to the marriage will lose the chance of acquiring.

(4) As regards the exercise of those powers in relation to a child of the family, the court shall in particular have regard to the matters mentioned in section 25(3)(a) to (e) of the 1973 Act.

(5) As regards the exercise of those powers against a party to the marriage in favour of a child of the family who is not the child of that party, the court shall also have regard to the matters mentioned in section 25(4)(a) to (c) of the 1973 Act.

(6)   Where an order has been made by a court outside England and Wales for the making of payments or the transfer of property by a party to the marriage, the court in considering in accordance with this section the financial resources of the other party to the marriage or a child of the family shall have regard to the extent to which that order has been complied with or is likely to be complied with.

(7)   In this section –

(a)   'pension arrangement' has the meaning given by section 25D(3) of the 1973 Act, and

(b)   references to benefits under a pension arrangement include any benefits by way of pension, whether under a pension arrangement or not.

19.   Consent orders for financial provision or property adjustment

(1)   Notwithstanding anything in section 18 above, on an application for a consent order for financial relief the court may, unless it has reason to think that there are other circumstances into which it ought to inquire, make an order in the terms agreed on the basis only of the prescribed information furnished with the application.

(2)   Subsection (1) above applies to an application for a consent order varying or discharging an order for financial relief as it applies to an application for an order for financial relief.

(3)   In this section –

'consent order', in relation to an application for an order, means an order in the terms applied for to which the respondent agrees;

'order for financial relief' means an order under section 17 above; and

'prescribed' means prescribed by rules of court.

20.   Restriction of powers of court where jurisdiction depends on matrimonial home in England or Wales

(1)   Where the court has jurisdiction to entertain an application for an order for financial relief by reason only of the situation in England or Wales of a dwelling-house which was a matrimonial home of the parties, the court may make under section 17 above any one or more of the following orders (but no other) –

(a)   an order that either party to the marriage shall pay to the other such lump sum as may be specified in the order;

(b)   an order that a party to the marriage shall pay to such person as may be so specified for the benefit of a child of the family, or to such a child, such lump sum as may be so specified;

(c) an order that a party to the marriage shall transfer to the other party, to any child of the family or to such person as may be so specified for the benefit of such a child, the interest of the first-mentioned party in the dwelling-house, or such part of that interest as may be so specified;

(d) an order that a settlement of the interest of a party to the marriage in the dwelling house, or such part of that interest as may be so specified, be made to the satisfaction of the court for the benefit of the other party to the marriage and of the children of the family or either or any of them;

(e) an order varying for the benefit of the parties to the marriage and of the children of the family or either or any of them any ante-nuptial or post-nuptial settlement (including such a settlement made by will or codicil) made on the parties to the marriage so far as that settlement relates to an interest in the dwelling-house;

(f) an order extinguishing or reducing the interest of either of the parties to the marriage under any such settlement so far as that interest is an interest in the dwelling-house;

(g) an order for the sale of the interest of a party to the marriage in the dwelling-house.

(2) Where, in the circumstances mentioned in subsection (1) above, the court makes an order for the payment of a lump sum by a party to the marriage, the amount of the lump sum shall not exceed, or where more than one such order is made the total amount of the lump sums shall not exceed in aggregate, the following amount, that is to say –

(a) if the interest of that party in the dwelling-house is sold in pursuance of an order made under subsection (1)(g) above, the amount of the proceeds of the sale of that interest after deducting therefrom any costs incurred in the sale thereof;

(b) if the interest of that party is not so sold, the amount which in the opinion of the court represents the value of that interest.

(3) Where the interest of a party to the marriage in the dwelling-house is held jointly or in common with any other person or persons –

(a) the reference in subsection (1)(g) above to the interest of a party to the marriage shall be construed as including a reference to the interest of that other person, or the interest of those other persons, in the dwelling-house, and

(b) the reference in subsection (2)(a) above to the amount of the proceeds of a sale ordered under subsection (1)(g) above shall be construed as a reference to that part of those proceeds which is attributable to the interest of that party of the marriage in the dwelling-house.

21. Application to orders under ss.14 and 17 of certain provisions of Part II of Matrimonial Causes Act 1973

(1) The following provisions of Part II of the 1973 Act (financial relief for parties to marriage and children of family) shall apply in relation to an order under section 14 or 17 above as they apply in relation to a like order under that Part of that Act, that is to say –

(a) section 23(3) (provisions as to lump sums);

(b) section 24A(2), (4), (5) and (6) (provisions as to order for sale);

(ba) section 24B(3) to (5) (provisions about pension sharing orders in relation to divorce and nullity);

(bb) section 24C (duty to stay pension sharing orders);

(bc) section 24D (apportionment of pension sharing charges);

(bd) section 25B(3) to (7B) (power, by financial provision order, to attach payments under a pension arrangement, or to require the exercise of a right of commutation under such an arrangement);

(be) section 25C (extension of lump sum powers in relation to death benefits under a pension arrangement);

(c) section 28(1) and (2) (duration of continuing financial provision orders in favour of party to marriage);

(d) section 29 (duration of continuing financial provision orders in favour of children, and age limit on making certain orders in their favour);

(e) section 30 (direction for settlement of instrument for securing payments or effecting property adjustment), except paragraph (b);

(f) section 31 (variation, discharge etc. of certain orders for financial relief), except subsection (2)(e) and subsection (4);

(g) section 32 (payment of certain arrears unenforceable without the leave of the court);

(h) section 33 (orders for repayment of sums paid under certain orders);

(i) section 38 (orders for repayment of sums paid after cessation of order by reason of remarriage);

(j) section 39 (settlements etc. made in compliance with a property adjustment order may be avoided on bankruptcy of settlor);

(k) section 40 (payments etc. under order made in favour of person suffering from mental disorder);

(l) section 40A (appeals relating to pension sharing orders which have taken effect).

(2) Subsection (1)(bd) and (be) above shall not apply where the court has jurisdiction to entertain an application for an order for financial relief by reason only of the situation in England or Wales of a dwelling-house which was a matrimonial home of the parties.

(3) Section 25D(1) of the 1973 Act (effect of transfers on order relating to rights under a pension arrangement) shall apply in relation to an order made under section 17 above by virtue of subsection (1)(bd) or (be) above as it applies in relation to an order made under section 23 of that Act by virtue of section 25B or 25C of the 1973 Act.

(4) The Lord Chancellor may by regulations make for the purposes of this Part of this Act provision corresponding to any provision which may be made by him under subsections (2) to (2B) of section 25D of the 1973 Act.

(5) Power to make regulations under this section shall be exercisable by statutory instrument which shall be subject to annulment in pursuance of a resolution of either House of Parliament.

22. Powers of the court in relation to certain tenancies of dwelling-houses

(1) This section applies if –

(a) an application is made by a party to a marriage for an order for financial relief; and

(b) one of the parties is entitled, either in his own right or jointly with the other party, to occupy a dwelling-house situated in England or Wales by virtue of a tenancy which is a relevant tenancy within the meaning of Schedule 7 to the Family Law Act 1996 (certain statutory tenancies).

(2) The court may make in relation to that dwelling-house any order which it could make under Part II of that schedule if a decree of divorce, a decree of nullity of marriage or a decree of judicial separation has been granted in England and Wales in respect of the marriage.

(3) The provisions of paragraphs 10, 11 and 14(1) in Part III of that Schedule apply in relation to any order under this section as they apply to any order under Part II of that Schedule.

Avoidance of transactions intended to prevent or reduce financial relief

23. Avoidance of transactions intended to defeat applications for financial relief

(1) For the purposes of this section 'financial relief' means relief under section 14 or 17 above and any reference to defeating a claim by a party to a marriage for financial relief is a reference to

preventing financial relief from being granted or reducing the amount of relief which might be granted, or frustrating or impeding the enforcement of any order which might be or has been made under either of those provisions at the instance of that party.

(2) Where leave is granted under section 13 above for the making by a party to a marriage of an application for an order for financial relief under section 17 above, the court may, on an application by that party –

   (a) if it is satisfied that the other party to the marriage is, with the intention of defeating the claim for financial relief, about to make any disposition or to transfer out of the jurisdiction or otherwise deal with any property, make such order as it thinks fit for restraining the other party from so doing or otherwise for protecting the claim;

   (b) if it is satisfied that the other party has, with that intention, made a reviewable disposition and that if the disposition were set aside financial relief or different financial relief would be granted to the applicant, make an order setting aside the disposition.

(3) Where an order for financial relief under section 14 or 17 above has been made by the court at the instance of a party to a marriage, then, on an application made by that party, the court may, if it is satisfied that the other party to the marriage has, with the intention of defeating the claim for financial relief, made a reviewable disposition, make an order setting aside the disposition.

(4) Where the court has jurisdiction to entertain the application for an order for financial relief by reason only of paragraph (c) of section 15(1) above, it shall not make any order under subsection (2) or (3) above in respect of any property other than the dwelling-house concerned.

(5) Where the court makes an order under subsection (2)(b) or (3) above setting aside a disposition it shall give such consequential directions as it thinks fit for giving effect to the order (including directions requiring the making of any payments or the disposal of any property).

(6) Any disposition made by the other party to the marriage (whether before or after the commencement of the application) is a reviewable disposition for the purposes of subsections (2)(b) and (3) above unless it was made for valuable consideration (other than marriage) to a person who, at the time of the disposition, acted in relation to it in good faith and without notice of any intention on the part of the other party to defeat the applicant's claim for financial relief.

(7) Where an application is made under subsection (2) or (3) above with respect to a disposition which took place less than three years before the date of the application or with respect to a disposition or other dealing with property which is about to take place and the court is satisfied –

    (a) in a case falling within subsection (2)(a) or (b) above, that the disposition or other dealing would (apart from this section) have the consequence, or

    (b) in a case falling within subsection (3) above, that the disposition has had the consequence,

of defeating a claim by the applicant for financial relief, it shall be presumed, unless the contrary is shown, that the person who disposed of or is about to dispose of or deal with the property did so or, as the case may be, is about to do so, with the intention of defeating the applicant's claim for financial relief.

(8) In this section 'disposition' does not include any provision contained in a will or codicil but, with that exception, includes any conveyance, assurance or gift of property of any description, whether made by an instrument or otherwise.

(9) The preceding provisions of this section are without prejudice to any power of the High Court to grant injunctions under section 37 of the Supreme Court Act 1981.

24. Prevention of transactions intended to defeat prospective applications for financial relief

(1) Where, on an application by a party to a marriage, it appears to the court –

    (a) that the marriage has been dissolved or annulled, or that the parties to the marriage have been legally separated, by means of judicial or other proceedings in an overseas country; and

    (b) that the applicant intends to apply for leave to make an application for an order for financial relief under section 17 above as soon as he or she has been habitually resident in England and Wales for a period of one year; and

    (c) that the other party to the marriage is, with the intention of defeating a claim for financial relief, about to make any disposition or to transfer out of the jurisdiction or otherwise deal with any property,

the court may make such order as it thinks fit for restraining the other party from taking such action as is mentioned in paragraph (c) above.

(2) For the purposes of an application under subsection (1) above –

(a) the reference to defeating a claim for financial relief shall be construed in accordance with subsection (1) of section 23 above (omitting the reference to any order which has been made); and

(b) subsections (7) and (8) of section 23 above shall apply as they apply for the purposes of an application under that section.

(3) The preceding provisions of this section are without prejudice to any power of the High Court to grant injunctions under section 37 of the Supreme Court Act 1981.

27. Interpretation of Part III

In this Part of this Act –

'the 1973 Act' means the Matrimonial Causes Act 1973;

'child of the family' has the same meaning as in section 52(1) of the 1973 Act;

'the court' means the High Court or, where a county court has jurisdiction by virtue of Part V of this Act, a county court;

'dwelling-house' includes any building or part thereof which is occupied as a dwelling, and any yard, garden, garage or outhouse belonging to the dwelling-house and occupied therewith;

'order for financial relief' has the meaning given by section 12(4) above;

'overseas country' means a country or territory outside the British Islands;

'possession' includes receipt of, or the right to receive, rents and profits;

'property adjustment order' means such an order as is specified in section 24(1)(a), (b), (c) or (d) of the 1973 Act;

'rent' does not include mortgage interest;

'secured periodical payments order' means such an order as is specified in section 23(1)(b) or (e) of the 1973 Act.

Welfare Reform and Pensions Act 1999

As amended by Child Support, Pensions and Social Security Act 2000, s.41.

PART III   PENSIONS ON DIVORCE ETC.

Pension sharing orders

19.   Orders in England and Wales

Schedule 3 (which amends the Matrimonial Causes Act 1973 for the purpose of enabling the court to make pension sharing orders in connection with proceedings in England and Wales for divorce or nullity of marriage, and for supplementary purposes) shall have effect.

Sections 25B to 25D of the Matrimonial Causes Act 1973

21.   Amendments

Schedule 4 (which amends the sections about pensions inserted in the Matrimonial Causes Act 1973 by section 166 of the Pensions Act 1995) shall have effect.

Miscellaneous

23.   Supply of pension information in connection with divorce etc.

(1)   The Secretary of State may by regulations –

   (a)   make provision imposing on the person responsible for a pension arrangement, or on the Secretary of State, requirements with respect to the supply of information relevant to any power with respect to –

      (i)   financial relief under Part II of the Matrimonial Causes Act 1973 or Part III of the Matrimonial and Family Proceedings Act 1984 (England and Wales powers in relation to domestic and overseas divorce etc.),

    (ii)   financial provision under the Family Law (Scotland) Act 1985 or Part IV of the Matrimonial and Family Proceedings Act 1984 (corresponding Scottish powers), or

    (iii)   financial relief under Part III of the Matrimonial Causes (Northern Ireland) Order 1978 or Part IV of the Matrimonial and Family Proceedings (Northern Ireland) Order 1989 (corresponding Northern Ireland powers);

(b)   make provision about calculation and vertification in relation to the valuation of –

    (i)   benefits under a pension arrangement, or

    (ii)   shareable state scheme rights,

for the purposes of regulations under paragraph (a)(i) or (iii);

(c)   make provision about calculation and verification in relation to –

    (i)   the valuation of shareable rights under a pension arrangement or shareable state scheme rights for the purposes of regulations under paragraph (a)(ii), so far as relating to the making of orders for financial provision (within the meaning of the Family Law (Scotland) Act 1985), or

    (ii)   the valuation of benefits under a pension arrangement for the purposes of such regulations, so far as relating to the making of orders under section 12A of that Act;

(d)   make provision for the purpose of enabling the person responsible for a pension arrangement to recover prescribed charges in respect of providing information in accordance with regulations under paragraph (a).

(2)   Regulations under subsection (1)(b) or (c) may include provision for calculation or verification in accordance with guidance from time to time prepared by a person prescribed by the regulations.

(3)   Regulations under subsection (1)(d) may include provision for the application in prescribed circumstances, with or without modification, of any provision made by virtue of section 41(2).

(4)   In subsection (1) –

(a)   the reference in paragraph (c)(i) to shareable rights under a pension arrangement is to rights in relation to which pension sharing is available under Chapter I of Part IV, or under corresponding Northern Ireland legislation, and

(b)   the references to shareable state scheme rights are to rights in relation to which pension sharing is available under Chapter II of Part IV, or under corresponding Northern Ireland legislation.

24.   Charges by pension arrangements in relation to earmarking orders

The Secretary of State may by regulations make provision for the purpose of enabling the person responsible for a pension arrangement to recover prescribed charges in respect of complying with –

(a)   an order under section 23 of the Matrimonial Causes Act 1973 (financial provision orders in connection with divorce etc.), so far as it includes provision made by virtue of section 25B or 25C of that Act (powers to include provision about pensions),

(b)   an order under section 12A(2) or (3) of the Family Law (Scotland) Act 1985 (powers in relation to pensions lump sums when making a capital sum order), or

(c)   an order under Article 25 of the Matrimonial Causes (Northern Ireland) Order 1978, so far as it includes provision made by virtue of Article 27B or 27C of that Order (Northern Ireland powers corresponding to those mentioned in paragraph (a)).

Supplementary

25.   Power to make consequential amendments of Part III

(1)   If any amendment by the Family Law Act 1996 of Part II or IV of the Matrimonial Causes Act 1973 comes into force before the day on which any provision of this Part comes into force, the Lord Chancellor may by order make such consequential amendment of that provision as he thinks fit.

(2)   No order under this section may be made unless a draft of the order has been laid before and approved by resolution of each House of Parliament.

26.   Interpretation of Part III

(1)   In this Part –

'occupational pension scheme' has the same meaning as in the Pension Schemes Act 1993;

'pension arrangement' means

(a)   an occupational pension scheme,

(b)   a personal pension scheme,

(c)   a retirement annuity contract,

(d)   an annuity or insurance policy purchases, or transferred, for the purpose of giving effect to rights under an occupational pension scheme or a personal pension scheme, and

(e)   an annuity purchased, or entered into, for the purpose of discharging liability in respect of a pension credit under section 29(1)(b) or under corresponding Northern Ireland legislation;

'personal pension scheme' has the same meaning as in the Pension Schemes Act 1993;

'prescribed' means prescribed by regulations made by the Secretary of State;

'retirement annuity contract' means a contract or scheme approved under Chapter III of Part XIV of the Income and Corporation Taxes Act 1988;

'trustees or managers', in relation to an occupational pension scheme or a personal pension scheme, means –

(a)   in the case of a scheme established under a trust, the trustees of the scheme, and

(b)   in any other case, the managers of the scheme.

(2)   References to the person responsible for a pension arrangement are –

(a)   in the case of an occupational pension scheme or a personal pension scheme, to the trustees or managers of the scheme,

(b)   in the case of a retirement annuity contract or an annuity falling within paragraph (d) or (e) of the definition of 'pension arrangement' above, the provider of the annuity, and

(c)   in the case of an insurance policy falling within paragraph (d) of the definition of that expression, the insurer.

PART IV   PENSION SHARING

CHAPTER I   SHARING OF RIGHTS UNDER PENSION ARRANGEMENTS

Pension sharing mechanism

27.   Scope of mechanism

(1)   Pension sharing is available under this Chapter in relation to a person's shareable rights under any pension arrangement other than an excepted public service pension scheme.

(2)   For the purposes of this Chapter, a person's shareable rights under a pension arrangement are any rights of his under the arrangement, other than rights of a description specified by regulations made by the Secretary of State.

(3)   For the purposes of subsection (1), a public service pension scheme is excepted if it is specified by order made by such Minister of the Crown or government department as may be designated by the Treasury as having responsibility for the scheme.

28.   Activation of pension sharing

(1)   Section 29 applies on the taking effect of any of the following relating to a person's shareable rights under a pension arrangement –

    (a)   a pension sharing order under the Matrimonial Causes Act 1973,

    (b)   provision which corresponds to the provision which may be made by such an order and which –

        (i)   is contained in a qualifying agreement between the parties to a marriage, and

        (ii)   takes effect on the dissolution of the marriage under the Family Law Act 1996,

    (c)   provision which corresponds to the provision which may be made by such an order and which –

        (i)   is contained in a qualifying agreement between the parties to a marriage or former marriage, and

        (ii)   takes effect after the dissolution of the marriage under the Family Law Act 1996,

    (d)   an order under Part III of the Matrimonial and Family Proceedings Act 1984 (financial relief in England and Wales in relation to overseas divorce etc.) corresponding to such an order as is mentioned in paragraph (a),

(e) a pension sharing order under the Family Law (Scotland) Act 1985,

(f) provision which corresponds to the provision which may be made by such an order and which –

    (i) is contained in a qualifying agreement between the parties to a marriage,

    (ii) is in such form as the Secretary of State may prescribe by regulations, and

    (iii) takes effect on the grant, in relation to the marriage, of decree of divorce under the Divorce (Scotland) Act 1976 or of declarator of nullity,

(g) an order under Part IV of the Matrimonial and Family Proceedings Act 1984 (financial relief in Scotland in relation to overseas divorce etc.) corresponding to such an order as is mentioned in paragraph (e),

(h) a pension sharing order under Northern Ireland legislation, and

(i) an order under Part IV of the Matrimonial and Family Proceedings (Northern Ireland) Order 1989 (financial relief in Northern Ireland in relation to overseas divorce etc.) corresponding to such an order as is mentioned in paragraph (h).

(2) For the purposes of subsection (1)(b) and (c), a qualifying agreement is one which –

(a) has been entered into in such circumstances as the Lord Chancellor may prescribe by regulations, and

(b) satisfies such requirements as the Lord Chancellor may so prescribe.

(3) For the purposes of subsection (1)(f), a qualifying agreement is one which –

(a) has been entered into in such circumstances as the Secretary of State may prescribe by regulations, and

(b) is registered in the Books of Council and Session.

(4) Subsection (1)(b) does not apply if –

(a) the pension arrangement to which the provision relates is the subject of a pension sharing order under the Matrimonial Causes Act 1973 in relation to the marriage, or

(b) there is in force a requirement imposed by virtue of section 25B or 25C of that Act (powers to include in financial provision orders requirements relating to benefits under pension arrangements) which relates to benefits or future benefits to which the party who is the transferor is entitled under the pension arrangement to which the provision relates.

(5) Subsection (1)(c) does not apply if –

    (a)   the marriage was dissolved by an order under section 3 of the Family Law Act 1996 (divorce not preceded by separation) and the satisfaction of the requirements of section 9(2) of that Act (settlement of future financial arrangements) was a precondition to the making of the order,

    (b)   the pension arrangement to which the provision relates –

        (i)   is the subject of a pension sharing order under the Matrimonial Causes Act 1973 in relation to the marriage, or

        (ii)   has already been the subject of pension sharing between the parties, or

    (c)   there is in force a requirement imposed by virtue of section 25B or 25C of that Act which relates to benefits or future benefits to which the party who is the transferor is entitled under the pension arrangement to which the provision relates.

(6) Subsection (1)(f) does not apply if there is in force an order under section 12A(2) or (3) of the Family Law (Scotland) Act 1985 which relates to benefits or future benefits to which the party who is the transferor is entitled under the pension arrangement to which the provision relates.

(7) For the purposes of this section, an order or provision falling within subsection (1)(e), (f) or (g) shall be deemed never to have taken effect if the person responsible for the arrangement to which the order or provision relates does not receive before the end of the period of 2 months beginning with the relevant date –

    (a)   copies of the relevant matrimonial documents, and

    (b)   such information relating to the transferor and transferee as the Secretary of State may prescribe by regulations under section 34(1)(b)(ii).

(8) The relevant date for the purposes of subsection (7) is –

    (a)   in the case of an order or provision falling within subsection (1)(e) or (f), the date of the extract of the decree or declarator responsible for the divorce or annulment to which the order or provision relates, and

(b) in the case of an order falling within subsection (1)(g), the date of disposal of the application under section 28 of the Matrimonial and Family Proceedings Act 1984.

(9) The reference in subsection (7)(a) to the relevant matrimonial documents is –

(a) in the case of an order falling within subsection (1)(e) or (g), to copies of the order and the order, decree or declarator responsible for the divorce or annulment to which it relates, and

(b) in the case of provision falling within subsection (1)(f), to –

(i) copies of the provision and the order, decree or declarator responsible for the divorce or annulment to which it relates, and

(ii) documentary evidence that the agreement containing the provision is one to which subsection (3)(a) applies.

(10) The sheriff may, on the application of any person having an interest, make an order –

(a) extending the period of 2 months referred to in subsection (7), and

(b) if that period has already expired, providing that, if the person responsible for the arrangement receives the documents and information concerned before the end of the period specified in the order, subsection (7) is to be treated as never having applied.

(11) In subsections (4)(b), (5)(c) and (6), the reference to the party who is the transferor is to the party to whose rights the provision relates.

29. Creation of pension debits and credits

(1) On the application of this section –

(a) the transferor's shareable rights under the relevant arrangement become subject to a debit of the appropriate amount, and

(b) the transferee becomes entitled to a credit of that amount as against the person responsible for that arrangement.

(2) Where the relevant order or provision specifies a percentage value to be transferred, the appropriate amount for the purposes of subsection (1) is the specified percentage of the cash equivalent of the relevant benefits on the valuation day.

(3) Where the relevant order or provision specifies an amount to be transferred, the appropriate amount for the purposes of subsection (1) is the lesser of –

    (a)   the specified amount, and

    (b)   the cash equivalent of the relevant benefits on the valuation day.

(4)   Where the relevant arrangement is an occupational pension scheme and the transferor is in pensionable service under the scheme on the transfer day, the relevant benefits for the purposes of subsections (2) and (3) are the benefits or future benefits to which he would be entitled under the scheme by virtue of his shareable rights under it had his pensionable service terminated immediately before that day.

(5)   Otherwise, the relevant benefits for the purposes of subsections (2) and (3) are the benefits or future benefits to which, immediately before the transfer day, the transferor is entitled under the terms of the relevant arrangement by virtue of his shareable rights under it.

(6)   The Secretary of State may by regulations provide for any description of benefit to be disregarded for the purposes of subsection (4) or (5).

(7)   For the purposes of this section, the valuation day is such day within the implementation period for the credit under subsection (1)(b) as the person responsible for the relevant arrangement may specify by notice in writing to the transferor and transferee.

(8)   In this section –

    'relevant arrangement' means the arrangement to which the relevant order or provision relates;

    'relevant order or provision' means the order or provision by virtue of which this section applies;

    'transfer day' means the day on which the relevant order or provision takes effect;

    'transferor' means the person to whose rights the relevant order or provision relates;

    'transferee' means the person for whose benefit the relevant order or provision is made.

30. Cash equivalents

(1)   The Secretary of State may by regulations make provision about the calculation and verification of cash equivalents for the purposes of section 29.

(2)   The power conferred by subsection (1) includes power to provide for calculation or verification –

(a) in such manner as may, in the particular case, be approved by a person prescribed by the regulations, or

(b) in accordance with guidance from time to time prepared by a person so prescribed.

Pension debits

31. Reduction of benefit

(1) Subject to subsection (2), where a person's shareable rights under a pension arrangement are subject to a pension debit, each benefit or future benefit –

(a) to which he is entitled under the arrangement by virtue of those rights, and

(b) which is a qualifying benefit,

is reduced by the appropriate percentage.

(2) Where a pension debit relates to the shareable rights under an occupational pension scheme of a person who is in pensionable service under the scheme on the transfer day, each benefit or future benefit –

(a) to which the person is entitled under the scheme by virtue of those rights, and

(b) which corresponds to a qualifying benefit,

is reduced by an amount equal to the appropriate percentage of the corresponding qualifying benefit.

(3) A benefit is a qualifying benefit for the purposes of subsections (1) and (2) if the cash equivalent by reference to which the amount of the pension debit is determined includes an amount in respect of it.

(4) The provisions of this section override any provision of a pension arrangement to which they apply to the extent that the provision conflicts with them.

(5) In this section –

'appropriate percentage', in relation to a pension debit, means –

(a) if the relevant order or provision specifies the percentage value to be transferred, that percentage;

(b) if the relevant order or provision specifies an amount to be transferred, the percentage which the appropriate amount for the purposes of subsection (1) of section 29 represents of the amount mentioned in subsection (3)(b) of that section;

'relevant order or provision', in relation to a pension debit, means the pension sharing order or provision on which the debit depends;

'transfer day', in relation to a pension debit, means the day on which the relevant order or provision takes effect.

32. Effect on contracted-out rights

(1) The Pension Schemes Act 1993 shall be amended as follows.

(2) In section 10 (protected rights), in subsection (1), for 'subsections (2) and (3)' there shall be substituted 'the following provisions of this section', and at the end there shall be added –

'(4) Where, in the case of a scheme which makes such provision as is mentioned in subsection (2) or (3), a member's rights under the scheme become subject to a pension debit, his protected rights shall exclude the appropriate percentage of the rights which were his protected rights immediately before the day on which the pension debit arose.

(5) For the purposes of subsection (4), the appropriate percentage is –

    (a) if the order or provision on which the pension debit depends specifies the percentage value to be transferred, that percentage;

    (b) if the order or provision on which the pension debit depends specifies an amount to be transferred, the percentage which the appropriate amount for the purposes of subsection (1) of section 29 of the Welfare Reform and Pensions Act 1999 (lessor of specified amount and cash equivalent of transferor's benefits) represents of the amount mentioned in subsection (3)(b) of that section (cash equivalent of transferor's benefits).'

(3) After section 15 there shall be inserted –

'15A Reduction of guaranteed minimum in consequence of pension debit

    (1) Where –

        (a) an earner has a guaranteed minimum in relation to the pension provided by a scheme, and

        (b) his right to the pension becomes subject to a pension debit, his guaranteed minimum in relation to the scheme is, subject to subsection (2), reduced by the appropriate percentage.

(2) Where the earner is in pensionable service under the scheme on the day on which the order or provision on which the pension debit depends takes effect, his guaranteed minimum in relation to the scheme is reduced by an amount equal to the appropriate percentage of the corresponding qualifying benefit.

(3) For the purposes of subsection (2), the corresponding qualifying benefit is the guaranteed minimum taken for the purpose of calculating the cash equivalent by reference to which the amount of the pension debit is determined.

(4) For the purposes of this section the appropriate percentage is –

   (a) if the order or provision on which the pension debit depends specifies the percentage value to be transferred, that percentage;

   (b) if the order or provision on which the pension debit depends specifies an amount to be transferred, the percentage which the appropriate amount for the purposes of subsection (1) of section 29 of the Welfare Reform and Pensions Act 1999 (lesser of specified amount and cash equivalent of transferor's benefits) represents of the amount mentioned in subsection (3)(b) of that section (cash equivalent of transferor's benefits).'

(4) In section 47 (entitlement to guaranteed minimum pensions for the purposes of the relationship with social security benefits), at the end there shall be added –

'(6) For the purposes of section 46, a person shall be treated as entitled to any guaranteed minimum pension to which he would have been entitled but for any reduction under section 15A.'

(5) In section 181(1), there shall be inserted at the appropriate place –

'pension debit' means a debit under section 29(1)(a) of the Welfare Reform and Pensions Act 1999;'.

Pension credits

33. Time for discharge of liability

(1)   A person subject to liability in respect of a pension credit shall discharge his liability before the end of the implementation period for the credit.

(2)   Where the trustees or managers of an occupational pension scheme have not done what is required to discharge their liability in respect of a pension credit before the end of the implementation period for the credit –

    (a)   they shall, except in such cases as the Secretary of State may prescribe by regulations, notify the Regulatory Authority of that fact within such period as the Secretary of State may so prescribe, and

    (b)   section 10 of the Pensions Act 1995 (power of the Regulatory Authority to impose civil penalties) shall apply to any trustee or manager who has failed to take all such steps as are reasonable to ensure that liability in respect of the credit was discharged before the end of the implementation period for it.

(3)   If trustees or managers to whom subsection (2)(a) applies fail to perform the obligation imposed by that provision, section 10 of the Pensions Act 1995 shall apply to any trustee or manager who has failed to take all reasonable steps to ensure that the obligation was performed.

(4)   On the application of the trustees or managers of an occupational pension scheme who are subject to liability in respect of a pension credit, the Regulatory Authority may extend the implementation period for the credit for the purposes of this section if it is satisfied that the application is made in such circumstances as the Secretary of State may prescribe by regulations.

(5)   In this section 'the Regulatory Authority' means the Occupational Pensions Regulatory Authority.

34. 'Implementation period'

(1)   For the purposes of this Chapter, the implementation period for a pension credit is the period of 4 months beginning with the later of –

    (a)   the day on which the relevant order or provision takes effect, and

    (b)   the first day on which the person responsible for the pension arrangement to which the relevant order or provision relates is in receipt of –

      (i)   the relevant matrimonial documents, and

     (ii)   such information relating to the transferor and transferee as the Secretary of State may prescribe by regulations.

(2)   The reference in subsection (1)(b)(i) to the relevant matrimonial documents is to copies of –

    (a)   the relevant order or provision, and

    (b)   the order, decree or declarator responsible for the divorce or annulment to which it relates,

and, if the pension credit depends on provision falling within subsection (1)(f) of section 28, to documentary evidence that the agreement containing the provision is one to which subsection (3)(a) of that section applies.

(3)   Subsection (1) is subject to any provision made by regulations under section 41(2)(a).

(4)   The Secretary of State may by regulations –

    (a)   make provision requiring a person subject to liability in respect of a pension credit to notify the transferor and transferee of the day on which the implementation period for the credit begins;

    (b)   provide for this section to have effect with modifications where the pension arrangement to which the relevant order or provision relates is being wound up;

    (c)   provide for this section to have effect with modifications where the pension credit depends on a pension sharing order and the order is the subject of an application for leave to appeal out of time.

(5)   In this section –

'relevant order or provision', in relation to a pension credit, means the pension sharing order or provision on which the pension credit depends;

'transferor' means the person to whose rights the relevant order or provision relates;

'transferee' means the person for whose benefit the relevant order or provision is made.

35. Mode of discharge of liability

(1)   Schedule 5 (which makes provision about how liability in respect of a pension credit may be discharged) shall have effect.

(2)   Where the person entitled to a pension credit dies before liability in respect of the credit has been discharged –

(a)   Schedule 5 shall cease to have effect in relation to the discharge of liability in respect of the credit, and

(b)   liability in respect of the credit shall be discharged in accordance with regulations made by the Secretary of State.

Treatment of pension credit rights under schemes

36.   Safeguarded rights

After section 68 of the Pension Schemes Act 1993 there shall be inserted –

'PART IIIA   SAFEGUARDED RIGHTS

68a.   Safeguarded rights

(1)   Subject to subsection (2), the safeguarded rights of a member of an occupational pension scheme or a personal pension scheme are such of his rights to future benefits under the scheme as are attributable (directly or indirectly) to a pension credit in respect of which the reference rights are, or include, contracted-out rights or safeguarded rights.

(2)   If the rules of an occupational pension scheme or a personal pension scheme so provide, a member's safeguarded rights are such of his rights falling within subsection (1) as –

(a)   in the case of rights directly attributable to a pension credit, represent the safeguarded percentage of the rights acquired by virtue of the credit, and

(b)   in the case of rights directly attributable to a transfer payment, represent the safeguarded percentage of the rights acquired by virtue of the payment.

(3)   For the purposes of subsection (2)(a), the safeguarded percentage is the percentage of the rights by reference to which the amount of the credit is determined which are contracted-out rights or safeguarded rights.

(4)   For the purposes of subsection (2)(b), the safeguarded percentage is the percentage of the rights in respect of which the transfer payment is made which are contracted-out rights or safeguarded rights.

(5)   In this section –

'contracted-out rights' means such rights under, or derived from –

(a)   an occupational pension scheme contracted-out by virtue of section 9(2) or (3), or

(b)   an appropriate personal pension scheme,

as may be prescribed;

'reference rights', in relation to a pension credit, means the rights by reference to which the amount of the credit is determined.

68B.   Requirements relating to safeguarded rights

Regulations may prescribe requirements to be met in relation to safeguarded rights by an occupational pension scheme or a personal pension scheme.

68C.   Reserve powers in relation to non-complying schemes

(1)   This section applies to –

(a)   any occupational pension scheme, other than a public service pension scheme, and

(b)   any personal pension scheme.

(2)   If any scheme to which this section applies does not comply with a requirement prescribed under section 68B and there are any persons who –

(a)   have safeguarded rights under the scheme, or

(b)   are entitled to any benefit giving effect to such rights under the scheme,

the Inland Revenue may direct the trustees or managers of the scheme to take or refrain from taking such steps as they may specify in writing for the purpose of safeguarding the rights of persons falling within paragraph (a) or (b).

(3)   A direction under subsection (2) shall be final and binding on the trustees or managers to whom the direction is given and any person claiming under them.

(4)   An appeal on a point of law shall lie to the High Court or, in Scotland, the Court of Session from a direction under subsection (2) at the instance of the trustees or managers, or any person claiming under them.

(5)   A direction under subsection (2) shall be enforceable –

(a)   in England and Wales, in a county court, as if it were an order of that court, and

(b)   in Scotland, by the sheriff, as if it were an order of the sheriff and whether or not the sheriff could himself have given such an order.

68D.   Power to control transfer or discharge of liability

Regulations may prohibit or restrict the transfer or discharge of any liability under an occupational pension scheme or a personal pension scheme in respect of safeguarded rights except in prescribed circumstances or on prescribed conditions.'

37.   Requirements relating to pension credit benefit

After section 101 of the Pension Schemes Act 1993 there shall be inserted –

'PART IVA   REQUIREMENTS RELATING TO PENSION CREDIT BENEFIT

CHAPTER I   PENSION CREDIT BENEFIT UNDER OCCUPATIONAL SCHEMES

101A.   Scope of Chapter I

(1)   This Chapter applies to any occupational pension scheme whose resources are derived in whole or part from –

    (a)   payments to which subsection (2) applies made or to be made by one or more employers of earners to whom the scheme applies, or

    (b)   such other payments by the earner or his employer, or both, as may be prescribed for different categories of scheme.

(2)   This subsection applies to payments –

    (a)   under an actual or contingent legal obligation, or

    (b)   in the exercise of a power conferred, or the discharge of a duty imposed, on a Minister of the Crown, government department or any other person, being a power or duty which extends to the disbursement or allocation of public money.

101B.   Interpretation

In this Chapter –

        'scheme' means an occupational pension scheme to which this Chapter applies;

        'pension credit rights' means rights to future benefits under a scheme which are attributable (directly or indirectly) to a pension credit;

'pension credit benefit', in relation to a scheme, means the benefits payable under the scheme to or in respect of a person by virtue of rights under the scheme attributable (directly or indirectly) to a pension credit;

'normal benefit age', in relation to a scheme, means the earliest age at which a person who has pension credit rights under the scheme is entitled to receive a pension by virtue of those rights (disregarding any scheme rule making special provision as to early payment of pension on ground of ill-health or otherwise).

101C.   Basic principle as to pension credit benefit

(1)   Normal benefit age under a scheme must be between 60 and 65.

(2)   A scheme must not provide for payment of pension credit benefit in the form of a lump sum at any time before normal benefit age, except in such circumstances as may be prescribed.

101D.   Form of pension credit benefit and its alternatives

(1)   Subject to subsection (2) and section 101E, a person's pension credit benefit under a scheme must be –

(a)   payable directly out of the resources of the scheme, or
(b)   assured to him by such means as may be prescribed.

(2)   Subject to subsections (3) and (4), a scheme may, instead of providing a person's pension credit benefit, provide –

(a)   for his pension credit rights under the scheme to be transferred to another occupational pension scheme or a person pension scheme with a view to acquiring rights for him under the rules of the scheme, or
(b)   for such alternatives to pension credit benefit as may be prescribed.

(3)   The option conferred by subsection (2)(a) is additional to any obligation imposed by Chapter II of this Part.

(4)   The alternatives specified in subsection (2)(a) and (b) may only be by way of complete or partial substitute for pension credit benefit –

(a)   if the person entitled to the benefit consents, or
(b)   in such other cases as may be prescribed.

101E. Discharge of liability where pension credit or alternative benefits secured by insurance policies or annuity contracts

(1) A transaction to which section 19 applies discharges the trustees or managers of a scheme from their liability to provide pension credit benefit or any alternative to pension credit benefit for or in respect of a member of the scheme if and to the extent that –

    (a) it results in pension credit benefit, or any alternative to pension credit benefit, for or in respect of the member being appropriately secured (within the meaning of that section),

    (b) the transaction is entered into with the consent of the member or, if the member has died, of the member's widow or widower, and

    (c) such requirements as may be prescribed are met.

(2) Regulations may provide that subsection (1)(b) shall not apply in prescribed circumstances.

CHAPTER II TRANSFER VALUES

101F. Power to give transfer notice

(1) An eligible member of a qualifying scheme may by notice in writing require the trustees or managers of the scheme to use an amount equal to the cash equivalent of his pension credit benefit for such one or more of the authorised purposes as he may specify in the notice.

(2) In the case of a member of an occupational pension scheme, the authorised purposes are –

    (a) to acquire rights allowed under the rules of an occupational pension scheme, or personal pension scheme, which is an eligible scheme,

    (b) to purchase from one or more insurance companies such as are mentioned in section 19(4)(a), chosen by the member and willing to accept payment on account of the member from the trustees or managers, one or more annuities which satisfy the prescribed requirements, and

    (c) in such circumstances as may be prescribed, to subscribe to other pension arrangements which satisfy prescribed requirements.

(3) In the case of a member of a personal pension scheme, the authorised purposes are –

(a) to acquire rights allowed under the rules of an occupational pension scheme, or personal pension scheme,
which is an eligible scheme, and

(b) in such circumstances as may be prescribed, to sub-
scribe to other pension arrangements which satisfy prescribed requirements.

(4) The cash equivalent for the purposes of subsection (1) shall –

(a) in the case of a salary related occupational pension
scheme, be taken to be the amount shown in the relevant
statement under section 101H, and

(b) in any other case, be determined by reference to the date
the notice under that subsection is given.

(5) The requirements which may be prescribed under subsection
(2) or (3) include, in particular, requirements of the Inland
Revenue.

(6) In subsections (2) and (3), references to an eligible scheme are
to a scheme –

(a) the trustees or managers of which are able and willing to
accept payment in respect of the members' pension
credit rights, and

(b) which satisfies the prescribed requirements.

(7) In this Chapter, 'transfer notice' means a notice under subsection (1).

101G. Restrictions on power to give transfer notice

(1) In the case of a salary related occupational pension scheme,
the power to give a transfer notice may only be exercised if –

(a) the member has been provided with a statement under
section 101H, and

(b) not more than 3 months have passed since the date by
reference to which the amount shown in the statement is
determined.

(2) The power to give a transfer notice may not be exercised in the
case of an occupational pension scheme if –

(a) there is less than a year to go until the member reaches
normal benefit age, or

(b) the pension to which the member is entitled by virtue
of his pension credit rights, or benefit in lieu of that
pension, or any part of it has become payable.

(3) Where an eligible member of a qualifying scheme –

    (a)   is entitled to make an application under section 95 to the trustees or managers of the scheme, or

    (b)   would be entitled to do so, but for the fact that he has not received a statement under section 93A in respect of which the guarantee date is sufficiently recent,

he may not, if the scheme so provides, exercise the power to give them a transfer notice unless he also makes an application to them under section 95.

  (4)   The power to give a transfer notice may not be exercised if a previous transfer notice given by the member to the trustees or managers of the scheme is outstanding.

101H.   Salary related schemes: statements of entitlement

  (1)   The trustees or managers of a qualifying scheme which is a salary related occupational pension scheme shall, on the application of an eligible member, provide him with a written statement of the amount of the cash equivalent of his pension credit benefit under the scheme.

  (2)   For the purposes of subsection (1), the amount of the cash equivalent shall be determined by reference to a date falling within –

    (a)   the prescribed period beginning with the date of the application, and

    (b)   the prescribed period ending with the date on which the statement under that subsection is provided to the applicant.

  (3)   Regulations may make provision in relation to applications under subsection (1) and may, in particular, restrict the making of successive applications.

  (4)   If trustees or managers to whom subsection (1) applies fail to perform an obligation under that subsection, section 10 of the Pensions Act 1995 (power of the Regulatory Authority to impose civil penalties) shall apply to any trustee or manager who has failed to take all such steps as are reasonable to secure that the obligation was performed.

101I.   Calculation of cash equivalents

Cash equivalents for the purposes of this Chapter shall be calculated and verified in the prescribed manner.

101J. Time for compliance with transfer notice

(1) Trustees or managers of a qualifying scheme who receive a transfer notice shall comply with the notice –

    (a) in the case of an occupational pension scheme, within 6 months of the valuation date or, if earlier, by the date on which the member to whom the notice relates reaches normal benefit age, and

    (b) in the case of a personal pension scheme, within 6 months of the date on which they receive the notice.

(2) The Regulatory Authority may, in prescribed circumstances, extend the period for complying with the notice.

(3) If the Regulatory Authority are satisfied –

    (a) that there has been a relevant change of circumstances since they granted an extension under subsection (2), or

    (b) that they granted an extension under that subsection in ignorance of a material fact or on the basis of a mistake as to a material fact,

that may revoke or reduce the extension.

(4) Where the trustees or managers of an occupational pension scheme have failed to comply with a transfer notice before the end of the period for compliance –

    (a) they shall, except in prescribed cases, notify the Regulatory Authority of that fact within the prescribed period, and

    (b) section 10 of the Pensions Act 1995 (power of the Regulatory Authority to impose civil penalties) shall apply to any trustee or manager who has failed to take all such steps as are reasonable to ensure that the notice was complied with before the end of the period for compliance.

(5) If trustees or manager to whom subsection (4)(a) applies fail to perform the obligation imposed by that provision, section 10 of the Pensions Act 1995 shall apply to any trustee or manager who has failed to take all such steps as are reasonable to ensure that the obligation was performed.

(6) Regulations may –

    (a) make provision in relation to applications under subsection (2), and

    (b) provide that subsection (4) shall not apply in prescribed circumstances.

(7) In this section, 'valuation date', in relation to a transfer notice given to the trustees or managers of an occupational pension scheme, means –

    (a) in the case of a salary related scheme, the date by reference to which the amount shown in the relevant statement under section 101H is determined, and

    (b) in the case of any other scheme, the date the notice is given.

101K. Withdrawal of transfer notice

(1) Subject to subsections (2) and (3), a person who have given a transfer notice may withdraw it by giving the trustees or managers to whom it was given notice in writing that he no longer requires them to comply with it.

(2) A transfer notice may not be withdrawn if the trustees or managers have already entered into an agreement with a third party to use the whole or part of the amount they are required to use in accordance with the notice.

(3) If the giving of a transfer notice depended on the making of an application under section 95, the notice may only be withdrawn if the application is also withdrawn.

101L. Variation of the amount required to be used

(1) Regulations may make provision for the amount required to be used under section 101F(1) to be reduced in prescribed circumstances.

(2) Without prejudice to the generality of subsection (1), the circumstances which may be prescribed include –

    (a) failure by the trustees or managers of a qualifying scheme to comply with a notice under section 101F(1) within 6 months of the date by reference to which the amount of the cash equivalent falls to be determined, and

    (b) the state of funding of a qualifying scheme.

(3) Regulations under subsection (1) may have the effect of extinguishing an obligation under section 101F(1).

101M. Effect of transfer on trustees' duties

Compliance with a transfer notice shall have effect to discharge the trustees or managers of a qualifying scheme from any obligation to provide the pension credit benefit of the eligible member who gave the notice.

101N. Matters to be disregarded in calculations

In making any calculation for the purposes of this Chapter –

    (a)   any charge or lien on, and

    (b)   any set-off against,

the whole or part of a pension shall be disregarded.

101O. Service of notices

A notice under section 101F(1) or 101K(1) shall be taken to have been given if it is delivered to the trustees or managers personally or sent by post in a registered letter or by recorded delivery service.

101P. Interpretation of Chapter II

    (1)   In this Chapter –

'eligible member', in relation to a qualifying scheme, means a member who has pension credit rights under the scheme;

'normal benefit age', in relation to an eligible member of a qualifying scheme, means the earliest age at which the member is entitled to receive a pension by virtue of his pension credit rights under the scheme (disregarding any scheme rule making special provision as to early payment of pension on grounds of ill-health or otherwise);

'pension credit benefit', in relation to an eligible member of a qualifying scheme, means the benefits payable under the scheme to or in respect of the member by virtue of rights under the scheme attributable (directly or indirectly) to a pension credit;

'pension credit rights', in relation to a qualifying scheme, means rights to future benefits under the scheme which are attributable (directly or indirectly) to a pension credit;

'qualifying scheme' means a funded occupational pension scheme and a personal pension scheme;

'transfer notice' has the meaning given by section 101F(7).

    (2)   For the purposes of this Chapter, an occupational pension scheme is salary related if –

        (a)   it is not a money purchase scheme, and

        (b)   it does not fall within a prescribed class.

(3) In this Chapter, references to the relevant statement under section 101H, in relation to a transfer notice given to the trustees or managers of a salary related occupational pension scheme, are to the statement under that section on which the giving of the notice depended.

(4) For the purposes of this section, an occupational pension scheme is funded it is meets its liabilities out of a fund accumulated for the purpose during the life of the scheme.

101Q. Power to modify Chapter II in relation to hybrid schemes

Regulations may apply this Chapter with prescribed modifications to occupational pension schemes –

> (a) which are not money purchase schemes, but
> (b) where some of the benefits that may be provided are money purchase benefits.'

38. Treatment in winding up

(1) In section 73 of the Pensions Act 1995 (treatment of rights on winding up of an occupational pension scheme to which section 56 of that Act (minimum funding requirement) applies), in subsection (3) (classification of liabilities), in paragraph (c) (accrued rights), at the end of sub-paragraph (i) there shall be inserted –

> '(ia) future pensions, or other future benefits, attributable (directly or indirectly) to pension credits (but excluding increased to pensions),'.

(2) In the case of an occupational pension scheme which is not a scheme to which section 56 of the Pensions Act 1995 applies, rights attributable (directly or indirectly) to a pension credit are to be accorded in a winding up the same treatment –

> (a) if they have come into payment, as the rights of a pensioner member, and
> (b) if they have not come into payment, as the rights of a deferred member.

(3) Subsection (2) overrides the provisions of a scheme to the extent that it conflicts with them, and the scheme has effect with such modifications as may be required in consequence.

(4) In subsection (2) –

> (a) 'deferred member' and 'pensioner member' have the same meanings as in Part I of the Pensions Act 1995,
> (b) 'pension credit' includes a credit under Northern Ireland legislation corresponding to section 29(1)(b), and

(c)   references to rights attributable to a pension credit having come into payment are to the person to whom the rights belong having become entitled by virtue of the rights to the present payment of pension or other benefits.

Indexation

39. Public service pension schemes

(1)   The Pensions (Increase) Act 1971 shall be amended as follows.

(2)   In section 3 (qualifying conditions), after subsection (2) there shall be inserted –

'(2A) A pension attributable to the pensioner having become entitled to a pension credit shall not be increased unless the pensioner has attained the age of fifty-five years.'

(3)   In section 8, in subsection (1) (definition of 'pension'), in paragraph (a), the words from '(either' to 'person)' shall be omitted.

(4)   In that section, in subsection (2) (when pension deemed for purposes of the Act to begin), after 'pension', in the first place, there shall be inserted 'which is not attributable to a pension credit', and after that subsection there shall be inserted –

'(2A) A pension which is attributable to a pension credit shall be deemed for purposes of this Act to begin on the day on which the order or provision on which the credit depends takes effect.'

(5)   In section 17(1) (interpretation) –

     (a)   for the definitions of 'derivative pension' and 'principal pension' there shall be substituted –

'"derivative pension" means a pension which –

         (a)   is not payable in respect of the pensioner's own services, and

         (b)   is not attributable to the pensioner having become entitled to a pension credit;',

     (b)   after the definition of 'pension' there shall be inserted –

'"pension credit" means a credit under section 29(1)(b) of the Welfare Reform and Pensions Act 1999 or under corresponding Northern Ireland legislation;

"principal pension" means a pension which –

         (a)   is payable in respect of the pensioner's own services, or

         (b)   is attributable to the pensioner having become entitled to a pension credit;', and

(c) for the definition of 'widow's pension' there shall be substituted –

'"widow's pension" means a pension payable –

    (a) in respect of the services of the pensioner's deceased husband, or

    (b) by virtue of the pensioner's deceased husband having become entitled to a pension credit.'

40. Other pension schemes

(1) The Secretary of State may by regulations make provision for a pension to which subsection (2) applies to be increased, as a minimum, by reference to increases in the retail prices index, so far as not exceeding 5% per annum.

(2) This subsection applies to –

    (a) a pension provided to give effect to eligible pension credit rights of a member under a qualifying occupational pension scheme, and

    (b) a pension provided to give effect to safeguarded rights of a member under a personal pension scheme.

(3) In this section –

'eligible', in relation to pension credit rights, means of a description prescribed by regulations made by the Secretary of State;

'pension credit rights', in relation to an occupational pension scheme, means rights to future benefits under the scheme which are attributable (directly or indirectly) to a credit under section 29(1)(b) or under corresponding Northern Ireland legislation;

'qualifying occupational pension scheme' means an occupational pension scheme which is not a public service pension scheme;

'safeguarded rights' has the meaning given in section 68A of the Pension Schemes Act 1993.

Charges by pension arrangements

41. Charges in respect of pension sharing costs

(1) The Secretary of State may by regulations make provision for the purpose of enabling the person responsible for a pension arrangement involved in pension sharing to recover from the

parties to pension sharing prescribed charges in respect of prescribed descriptions of pension sharing activity.

(2) Regulations under subsection (1) may include:

    (a) provision for the start of the implementation period for a pension credit to be postponed in prescribed circumstances;

    (b) provision, in relation to payments in respect of charges recoverable under the regulations, for reimbursement as between the parties to pension sharing;

    (c) provision, in relation to the recovery of charges by deduction from a pension credit, for the modification of Schedule 5;

    (d) provision for the recovery in prescribed circumstances of such additional amounts as may be determined in accordance with the regulations.

(3) For the purposes of regulations under subsection (1), the question of how much of a charge recoverable under the regulations is attributable to a party to pension sharing is to be determined as follows –

    (a) where the relevant order or provision includes provision about the apportionment of charges under this section, there is attributable to the party so much of the charge as is apportioned to him by that provision;

    (b) where the relevant order or provision does not include such provision, the charge is attributable to the transferor.

(4) For the purposes of subsection (1), a pension arrangement is involved in pension sharing if section 29 applies by virtue of an order or provision which relates to the arrangement.

(5) In that subsection, the reference to pension sharing activity is to activity attributable (directly or indirectly) to the involvement in pension sharing.

(6) In subsection (3) –

    (a) the reference to the relevant order or provision is to the order or provision which gives rise to the pension sharing, and

    (b) the reference to the transferor is to the person to whose rights that order or provision relates.

(7) In this section 'prescribed' means prescribed in regulations under subsection (1).

Adaptation of statutory schemes

42. Extension of scheme-making powers

(1) Power under an Act to establish a pension scheme shall include power to make provision for the provision, by reference to pension credits which derive from rights under –

(a)   the scheme, or

(b)   a scheme in relation to which the scheme is specified as an alternative for the purposes of paragraph 2 of Schedule 5,

of benefits to or in respect of those entitled to the credits.

(2)   Subsection (1) is without prejudice to any other power.

(3)   Subsection (1) shall apply in relation to Acts whenever passed.

(4)   No obligation to consult shall apply in relation to the making, in exercise of a power under an Act to establish a pension scheme, of provision of a kind authorised by subsection (1).

(5)   Any provision of, or under, an Act which makes benefits under a pension scheme established under an Act a charge on, or payable out of –

(a)   the Consolidated Fund,

(b)   the Scottish Consolidated Fund, or

(c)   the Consolidated Fund of Northern Ireland,

shall be treated as including any benefits under the scheme which are attributable (directly or indirectly) to a pension credit which derives from rights to benefits charged on, or payable out of, that fund.

(6)   In this section –

'pension credit' includes a credit under Northern Ireland legislation corresponding to section 29(1)(b);

'pension scheme' means a scheme or arrangement providing benefits, in the form of pensions or otherwise, payable on termination of service, or on death or retirement, to or in respect of persons to whom the scheme or arrangement applies.

43.   Power to extend judicial pension schemes

(1)   The appropriate minister may by regulations amend the Sheriffs' Pensions (Scotland) Act 1961, the Judicial Pensions Act 1981 or the Judicial Pensions and Retirement Act 1993 for the purpose of –

(a)   extending a pension scheme under the Act to include the provision, by reference to pension credits which derive from rights under –

(i)   the scheme, or

(ii)   a scheme in relation to which the scheme is specified as an alternative for the purposes of paragraph 2 of Schedule 5,

of benefits to or in respect of those entitled to the credits, or

    (b)   restricting the power of the appropriate minister to accept payments into a pension scheme under the Act, where the payments represent the cash equivalent of rights under another pension scheme which are attributable (directly or indirectly) to a pension credit.

(2)   Regulations under subsection (1) –

    (a)   may make benefits provided by virtue of paragraph (a) of that subsection a charge on, and payable out of, the Consolidated Fund;

    (b)   may confer power to make subordinate legislation, including subordinate legislation which provides for calculation of the value of rights in accordance with guidance from time to time prepared by a person specified in the subordinate legislation.

(3)   The appropriate minister for the purposes of subsection (1) is –

    (a)   in relation to a pension scheme whose ordinary members are limited to those who hold judicial office whose jurisdiction is exercised exclusively in relation to Scotland, the Secretary of State, and

    (b)   in relation to any other pension scheme, the Lord Chancellor.

(4)   In this section –

'pension credit' includes a credit under Northern Ireland legislation corresponding to section 29(1)(b);

'pension scheme' means a scheme or arrangement providing benefits, in the form of pensions or otherwise, payable on termination of service, or on death or retirement, to or in respect of persons to whom the scheme or arrangement applies.

Supplementary

44. Disapplication of restrictions on alienation

(1)   Nothing in any of the following provisions (restrictions on alienation of pension rights) applies in relation to any order or provision falling within section 28(1) –

    (a)   section 203(1) and (2) of the Army Act 1955, section 203(1) and (2) of the Air Force Act 1955, section 128G(1) and (2) of the Naval Discipline Act 1957 and section 159(4) and (4A) of the Pension Schemes Act 1993,

    (b)   section 91 of the Pensions Act 1995,

(c) any provision of any enactment (whether passed or made before or after this Act is passed) corresponding to any of the enactments mentioned in paragraphs (a) and (b), and

(d) any provision of a pension arrangement corresponding to any of those enactments.

(2) In this section, 'enactment' includes an enactment comprised in subordinate legislation (within the meaning of the Interpretation Act 1978).

45. Information

(1) The Secretary of State may by regulations require the person responsible for a pension arrangement involved in pension sharing to supply to such persons as he may specify in the regulations such information relating to anything which follows from the application of section 29 as he may so specify.

(2) Section 168 of the Pension Schemes Act 1993 (breach of regulations) shall apply as if this section were contained in that Act (otherwise than in Chapter II of Part VII).

(3) For the purposes of this section, a pension arrangement is involved in pension sharing if section 29 applies by virtue of an order or provision which relates to the arrangement.

46. Interpretation of Chapter I

(1) In this Chapter –

'implementation period', in relation to a pension credit, has the meaning given by section 34;

'occupational pension scheme' has the meaning given by section 1 of the Pension Schemes Act 1993;

'pension arrangement' means –

(a) an occupational pension scheme,

(b) a personal pension scheme,

(c) a retirement annuity contract,

(d) an annuity or insurance policy purchased, or transferred, for the purpose of giving effect to rights under an occupational pension scheme or a personal pension scheme, and

(e) an annuity purchased, or entered into, the the purpose of discharging liability in respect of a credit under section 29(1)(b) or under corresponding Northern Ireland legislation;

'pension credit', means a credit under section 29(1)(b);

'pension debit' means a debit under section 29(1)(a);

'pensionable service', in relation to a member of an occupational pension scheme, means service in any description or category of employment to which the scheme relates which qualifies the member (on the assumption that it continues for the appropriate period) for pension or other benefits under the scheme;

'personal pension scheme' has the meaning given by section 1 of the Pension Schemes Act 1993;

'retirement annuity contract' means a contract or scheme approved under Chapter III of Part XIV of the Income and Corporation Taxes Act 1988;

'shareable rights' has the meaning given by section 27(2);

'trustees or managers', in relation to an occupational pension scheme or a personal pension scheme means –

(a) in the case of a scheme established under a trust, the trustees of the scheme, and

(b) in any other case, the managers of the scheme.

(2) In this Chapter, references to the person responsible for a pension arrangement are –

(a) in the case of an occupational pension scheme or a personal pension scheme, to the trustees or managers of the scheme,

(b) in the case of a retirement annuity contract or an annuity falling within paragraph (d) or (e) of the definition of 'pension arrangement' in subsection (1), to the provider of the annuity, and

(c) in the case of an insurance policy falling within paragraph (d) of the definition of that expression, to the insurer.

(3) In determining what is 'pensionable service' for the purposes of this Chapter –

(a) service notionally attributable for any purpose of the scheme is to be disregarded, and

(b) no account is to be taken of any rules of the scheme by which a period of service can be treated for any purpose as being longer or shorter than it actually is.

CHAPTER II SHARING OF STATE SCHEME RIGHTS

47. Shareable state scheme rights

(1) Pension sharing is available under this Chapter in relation to a person's shareable state scheme rights.

(2) For the purposes of this Chapter, a person's shareable state scheme rights are –

    (a) his entitlement, or prospective entitlement, to a Category A retirement pension by virtue of section 44(3)(b) of the Contributions and Benefits Act (earnings-related additional pension), and

    (b) his entitlement, or prospective entitlement, to a pension under section 55A of that Act (shared additional pension).

48. Activation of benefit sharing

(1) Section 49 applies on the taking effect of any of the following relating to a person's shareable state scheme rights –

    (a) a pension sharing order under the Matrimonial Causes Act 1973,

    (b) provision which corresponds to the provision which may be made by such an order and which –

        (i) is contained in a qualifying agreement between the parties to a marriage, and

        (ii) takes effect on the dissolution of the marriage under the Family Law Act 1996,

    (c) provision which corresponds to the provision which may be made by such an order and which –

        (i) is contained in a qualifying agreement between the parties to a marriage or former marriage, and

        (ii) takes effect after the dissolution of the marriage under the Family Law Act 1996,

    (d) an order under Part III of the Matrimonial and Family Proceedings Act 1984 (financial relief in England and Wales in relation to overseas divorce etc.) corresponding to such an order as is mentioned in paragraph (a),

    (e) a pension sharing order under the Family Law (Scotland) Act 1985,

    (f) provision which corresponds to the provision which may be made by such an order and which –

      (i)   is contained in a qualifying agreement between the parties to a marriage,

     (ii)   is in such form as the Secretary of State may prescribe by regulations, and

    (iii)   takes effect on the grant, in relation to the marriage, of decree of divorce under the Divorce (Scotland) Act 1976 or of declarator of nullity,

  (g)   an order under Part IV of the Matrimonial and Family Proceedings Act 1984 (financial relief in Scotland in relation to overseas divorce etc.) corresponding to such an order as is mentioned in paragraph (e),

  (h)   a pension sharing order under Northern Ireland legislation, and

  (i)   an order under Part IV of the Matrimonial and Family Proceedings (Northern Ireland) Order 1989 (financial relief in Northern Ireland in relation to overseas divorce etc.) corresponding to such an order as is mentioned in paragraph (h).

(2)   For the purposes of subsection (1)(b) and (c), a qualifying agreement is one which –

  (a)   has been entered into in such circumstances as the Lord Chancellor may prescribe by regulations, and

  (b)   satisfies such requirements as the Lord Chancellor may so prescribe.

(3)   For the purposes of subsection (1)(f), a qualifying agreement is one which –

  (a)   has been entered into in such circumstances as the Secretary of State may prescribe by regulations, and

  (b)   is registered in the Books of Council and Session.

(4)   Subsection (1)(b) does not apply if the provision relates to rights which are the subject of a pension sharing order under the Matrimonial Causes Act 1973 in relation to the marriage.

(5)   Subsection (1)(c) does not apply if –

  (a)   the marriage was dissolved by an order under section 3 of the Family Law Act 1996 (divorce not preceded by separation) and the satisfaction of the requirements of section 9(2) of that Act (settlement of future financial arrangements) was a precondition to the making of the order,

  (b)   the provision relates to rights which are the subject of a pension sharing order under the Matrimonial Causes Act 1973 in relation to the marriage, or

(c) shareable state scheme rights have already been the subject of pension sharing between the parties.

(6) For the purposes of this section, an order or provision falling within subsection (1)(e), (f) or (g) shall be deemed never to have taken effect if the Secretary of State does not receive before the end of the period of 2 months beginning with the relevant date –

(a) copies of the relevant matrimonial documents, and

(b) such information relating to the transferor and transferee as the Secretary of State may prescribe by regulations under section 34(1)(b)(ii).

(7) The relevant date for the purposes of subsection (6) is –

(a) in the case of an order or provision falling within subsection (1)(e) or (f), the date of the extract of the decree of declarator responsible for the divorce or annulment to which the order or provision relates, and

(b) in the case of an order falling within subsection (1)(g), the date of disposal of the application under section 28 of the Matrimonial and Family Proceedings Act 1984.

(8) The reference in subsection (6)(a) to the relevant matrimonial documents is –

(a) in the case of an order falling within subsection (1)(e) or (g), to copies of the order and the order, decree or declarator responsible for the divorce or annulment to which it relates, and

(b) in the case of the provision falling within subsection (1)(f), to –

(i) copies of the provision and the order, decree or declarator responsible for the divorce or annulment to which it relates, and

(ii) documentary evidence that the agreement containing the provision is one to which subsection (3)(a) applies.

(9) The sheriff may, on the application of any person having an interest, make an order –

(a) extending the period of 2 months referred to in subsection (6), and

(b) if that period has already expired, providing that, if the Secretary of State receives the documents and information concerned before the end of the period specified in the order, subsection (6) is to be treated as never having applied.

49. Creation of state scheme pension debits and credits

(1) On the application of this section –

    (a) the transferor becomes subject, for the purposes of Part II of the Contributions and Benefits Act (contributory benefits), to a debit of the appropriate amount, and

    (b) the transferee becomes entitled, for those purposes, to a credit of that amount.

(2) Where the relevant order or provision specifies a percentage value to be transferred, the appropriate amount for the purposes of subsection (1) is the specified percentage of the cash equivalent on the transfer day of the transferor's shareable state scheme rights immediately before that day.

(3) Where the relevant order or provision specifies an amount to be transferred, the appropriate amount for the purposes of subsection (1) is the lesser of –

    (a) the specified amount, and

    (b) the cash equivalent on the transfer day of the transferor's relevant state scheme rights immediately before that day.

(4) The Secretary of State may by regulations make provision about the calculation and verification of cash equivalents for the purposes of this section.

(4A) The power conferred by subsection (4) above includes power to provide –

    (a) for calculation or verification in such manner as may be approved by or on behalf of the Government Actuary, and

    (b) for things done under the regulations to be required to be done in accordance with guidance from time to time prepared by a person prescribed by the regulations.

(5) In determining prospective entitlement to a Category A retirement pension for the purposes of this section, only tax years before that in which the transfer day falls shall be taken into account.

(6) In this section –

'relevant order or provision' means the order or provision by virtue of which this section applies;

'transfer day' means the day on which the relevant order or provision takes effect;

'transferor' means the person to whose rights the relevant order or provision relates;

'transferee' means the person for whose benefit the relevant order or provision is made.

170

50. Effect of state scheme pension debits and credits

(1) Schedule 6 (which amends the Contributions and Benefits Act for the purpose of giving effect to debits and credits under section 49(1)) shall have effect.

(2) Section 55C of that Act (which is inserted by that Schedule) shall have effect, in relation to incremental periods (within the meaning of that section) beginning on or after 6th April 2010, with the following amendments –

    (a) in subsection (3), for 'period of enhancement' there is substituted 'period of deferment',

    (b) in subsection (4), for '1/7th per cent.' there is substituted '1/5th per cent.',

    (c) in subsection (7), for 'period of enhancement', in both places, there is substituted 'period of deferment', and

    (d) in subsection (9), the definition of 'period of enhancement' (and the preceding 'and') are omitted.

51. Interpretation of Chapter II

In this Chapter –

    'shareable state scheme rights' has the meaning given by section 47(2); and

    'tax year' has the meaning given by section 122(1) of the Contributions and Benefits Act.

SCHEDULE 5   PENSIONS CREDITS: MODE OF DISCHARGE

Funded pension schemes

1. (1) This paragraph applies to a pension credit which derives from –

    (a) a funded occupational pension scheme, or

    (b) a personal pension scheme.

(2) The trustees or managers of the scheme from which a pension credit to which this paragraph applies derives may discharge their liability in respect of the credit by conferring appropriate rights under that scheme on the person entitled to the credit –

    (a) with his consent, or

    (b) in accordance with regulations made by the Secretary of State.

(3) The trustees or managers of the scheme from which a pension credit to which this paragraph applies derives may discharge their liability in respect of the credit by paying the amount of the credit

to the person responsible for a qualifying arrangement with a view to acquiring rights under that arrangement for the person entitled to the credit if –

(a) the qualifying arrangement is not disqualified as a destination for the credit,

(b) the person responsible for that arrangement is able and willing to accept payment in respect of the credit, and

(c) payment is made with the consent of the person entitled to the credit, or in accordance with regulations made by the Secretary of State.

(4) For the purposes of sub-paragraph (2), no account is to be taken of consent of the person entitled to the pension credit unless –

(a) it is given after receipt of notice in writing of an order to discharge liability in respect of the credit by making a payment under sub-paragraph (3), or

(b) it is not withdrawn within 7 days of receipt of such notice.

Unfunded public service pension schemes

2. (1) This paragraph applies to a pension credit which derives from an occupational pension scheme which is –

(a) not funded, and

(b) a public service pension scheme.

(2) The trustees or managers of the scheme from which a pension credit to which this paragraph applies derives may discharge their liability in respect of the credit by conferring appropriate rights under that scheme on the person entitled to the credit.

(3) If such a scheme as is mentioned in sub-paragraph (1) is closed to new members, the appropriate authority in relation to that scheme may by regulations specify another public service pension scheme as an alternative to it for the purposes of this paragraph.

(4) Where the trustees or managers of a scheme in relation to which an alternative is specified under sub-paragraph (3) are subject to liability in respect of a pension credit, they may –

(a) discharge their liability in respect of the credit by securing that appropriate rights are conferred on the person entitled to the credit by the trustees or managers of the alternative scheme, and

(b) for the purpose of so discharging their liability, require the trustees or managers of the alternative scheme to take such steps as may be required.

(5) In sub-paragraph (3), 'the appropriate authority', in relation to a public service pension scheme, means such Minister of the Crown or government department as may be designated by the Treasury as having responsibility for the scheme.

Other unfunded occupational pension schemes

3. (1) This paragraph applies to a pension credit which derives from an occupational pension scheme which is –

(a) not funded, and
(b) not a public service pension scheme.

(2) The trustees or managers of the scheme from which a pension credit to which this paragraph applies derives may discharge their liability in respect of the credit by conferring appropriate rights under that scheme on the person entitled to the credit.

(3) The trustees or managers of the scheme from which a pension credit to which this paragraph applies derives may discharge their liability in respect of the credit by paying the amount of the credit to the person responsible for a qualifying arrangement with a view to acquiring rights under that arrangement for the person entitled to the credit if –

(a) the qualifying arrangement is not disqualified as a destination for the credit,
(b) the person responsible for that arrangement is able and willing to accept payment in respect of the credit, and
(c) payment is made with the consent of the person entitled to the credit, or in accordance with regulations made by the Secretary of State.

Other pension arrangements

4. (1) This paragraph applies to a pension credit which derives from –

(a) a retirement annuity contract,
(b) an annuity or insurance policy purchased or transferred for the purpose of giving effect to rights under an occupational pension scheme or a personal pension scheme, or
(c) an annuity purchased, or entered into, for the purpose of discharging liability in respect of a pension credit.

(2) The person responsible for the pension arrangement from which a pension credit to which this paragraph applies derives may discharge his liability in respect of the credit by paying the amount of the credit to the person responsible for a qualifying arrangement with a view to acquiring rights under that arrangement for the person entitled to the credit if –

(a) the qualifying arrangement is not disqualified as a destination for the credit,

(b) the person responsible for that arrangement is able and willing to accept payment in respect of the credit, and

(c) payment is made with the consent of the person entitled to the credit, or in accordance with regulations made by the Secretary of State.

(3) The person responsible for the pension arrangement from which a pension credit to which this paragraph applies derives may discharge his liability in respect of the credit by entering into an annuity contract with the person entitled to the credit if the contract is not disqualified as a destination for the credit.

(4) The person responsible for the pension arrangement from which a pension credit to which this paragraph applies derives may, in such circumstances as the Secretary of State may prescribe by regulations, discharge his liability in respect of the credit by assuming an obligation to provide an annuity for the person entitled to the credit.

(5) In sub-paragraph (1)(c), 'pension credit' includes a credit under Northern Ireland legislation corresponding to section 29(1)(b).

Appropriate rights

5. For the purposes of this Schedule, rights conferred on the person entitled to a pension credit are appropriate if –

(a) they are conferred with effect from, and including, the day on which the order, or provision, under which the credit arises takes effect, and

(b) their value, when calculated in accordance with regulations made by the Secretary of State, equals the amount of the credit.

Qualifying arrangements

6. (1) The following are qualifying arrangements for the purposes of this Schedule –

(a) an occupational pension scheme,

(b) a personal pension scheme,

(c) an appropriate annuity contract,

(d) an appropriate policy of insurance, and

(e) an overseas arrangement within the meaning of the Contracting-out (Transfer and Transfer Payment) Regulations 1996.

(2) An annuity contract or policy of insurance is appropriate for the purposes of sub-paragraph (1) if, at the time it is entered into or taken out, the insurance company with which it is entered into or taken out –

    (a) is carrying on ordinary long-term insurance business in the United Kingdom or any other member State, and

    (b) satisfies such requirements as the Secretary of State may prescribe by regulations.

(3) In this paragraph, 'ordinary long-term insurance business' has the same meaning as in the Insurance Companies Act 1982.

Disqualification as destination for pension credit

7. (1) If a pension credit derives from a pension arrangement which is approved for the purposes of Part XIV of the Income and Corporation Taxes Act 1988, an arrangement is disqualified as a destination for the credit unless –

    (a) it is also approved for those purposes, or

    (b) it satisfies such requirements as the Secretary of State may prescribe by regulations.

(2) If the rights by reference to which the amount of a pension credit is determined are or include contracted-out rights or safeguarded rights, an arrangement is disqualified as a destination for the credit unless –

    (a) it is of a description prescribed by the Secretary of State by regulations, and

    (b) it satisfies such requirements as he may so prescribe.

(3) An occupational pension scheme is disqualified as a destination for a pension credit unless the rights to be acquired under the arrangement by the person entitled to the credit are rights whose value, when calculated in accordance with regulations made by the Secretary of State, equals the credit.

(4) An annuity contract of insurance policy is disqualified as a destination for a pension credit in such circumstances as the Secretary of State may prescribe by regulations.

(5) The requirements which may be prescribed under sub-paragraph (1)(b) include, in particular, requirements of the Inland Revenue.

(6) In sub-paragraph (2) –

'contracted-out rights' means such rights under, or derived from –

    (a) an occupational pension scheme contracted-out by virtue of section 9(2) or (3) of the Pension Schemes Act 1993, or

(b) a personal pension scheme which is an appropriate scheme for the purposes of that Act,

as the Secretary of State may prescribe by regulations;

'safeguarded rights' has the meaning given by section 68A of the Pension Schemes Act 1993.

Adjustments to amount of pension credit

8. (1) If –

    (a) a pension credit derives from an occupational pension scheme,

    (b) the scheme is one to which section 56 of the Pensions Act 1995 (minimum funding requirement for funded salary related schemes) applies,

    (c) the scheme is underfunded on the valuation day, and

    (d) such circumstances as the Secretary of State may prescribe by regulations apply,

paragraph 1(3) shall have effect in relation to the credit as if the reference to the amount of the credit were to such lesser amount as may be determined in accordance with regulations made by the Secretary of State.

    (2) Whether a scheme is underfunded for the purposes of sub-paragraph (1)(c) shall be determined in accordance with regulations made by the Secretary of State.

    (3) For the purposes of that provision, the valuation day is the day by reference to which the cash equivalent on which the amount of the pension credit depends falls to be calculated.

9. If –

    (a) a person's shareable rights under a pension arrangement have become subject to a pension debit, and

    (b) the person responsible for the arrangement makes a payment which is referable to those rights without knowing of the pension debit,

this Schedule shall have effect as if the amount of the corresponding pension credit were such lesser amount as may be determined in accordance with regulations made by the Secretary of State.

10. The Secretary of State may by regulations make provision for paragraph 1(3), 3(3) or 4(2) to have effect, where payment is made after the end of the implementation period for the pension credit, as if the reference to the amount of the credit were to such larger amount as may be determined in accordance with the regulations.

General

11. Liability in respect of a pension credit shall be treated as discharged if the effect of paragraph 8(1) or 9 is to reduce it to zero.

12. Liability in respect of a pension credit may not be discharged otherwise than in accordance with this Schedule.

13. Regulations under paragraph 5(6) or 7(3) may provide for calculation of the value of rights in accordance with guidance from time to time prepared by a person specified in the regulations.

14. In this Schedule –

'funded', in relation to an occupational pension scheme, means that the scheme meets its liabilities out of a fund accumulated for the purpose during the life of the scheme;

'public service pension scheme' has the same meaning as in the Pension Schemes Act 1993.

SCHEDULE 6   EFFECT OF STATE SCHEME PENSION DEBITS AND CREDITS

1. The Contributions and Benefits Act is amended as follows.

2. After section 45A there is inserted –

'45B.   Reduction of additional pension in Category A retirement pension: pension sharing

    (1)   The weekly rate of the additional pension in a Category A retirement pension shall be reduced as follows in any case where –

        (a)   the pensioner has become subject to a state scheme pension debit, and

        (b)   the debit is to any extent referable to the additional pension.

    (2)   If the pensioner became subject to the debit in or after the final relevant year, the weekly rate of the additional pension shall be reduced by the appropriate weekly amount.

    (3)   If the pensioner became subject to the debit before the final relevant year, the weekly rate of the additional pension shall be reduced by the appropriate weekly amount multiplied by the relevant revaluation percentage.

    (4)   The appropriate weekly amount for the purposes of subsection (2) and (3) above is the weekly rate, expressed in terms of the valuation day, at which the cash equivalent, on that day, of the pension mentioned in subsection (5) below is equal to so much of the debit as is referable to the additional pension

(5) The pension referred to above is a notional pension for the pensioner by virtue of section 44(3)(b) above which becomes payable on the later of –

    (a)   his attaining pensionable age, and

    (b)   the valuation day.

(6) For the purposes of subsection (3) above, the relevant revaluation percentage is the percentage specified, in relation to earnings factors for the tax year in which the pensioner became subject to the debit, by the last order under section 148 of the Administration Act to come into force before the end of the final relevant year.

(7) Cash equivalents for the purposes of this section shall be calculate in accordance with regulations.

(8) In this section –

    "final relevant year" means the tax year immediately preceding that in which the pensioner attains pensionable age;

    "state scheme pension debit" means a debit under section 49(1)(a) of the Welfare Reform and Pensions Act 1999 (debit for the purposes of this Part of this Act);

    "valuation day" means the day on which the pensioner became subject to the state scheme pension debit.'

3.   After section 55 there is inserted –

'Shared additional pension

55A. Shared additional pension

(1) A person shall be entitled to a shared additional pension if he is –

    (a)   over pensionable age, and

    (b)   entitled to a state scheme pension credit.

(2) A person's entitlement to a shared additional pension shall continue throughout his life.

(3) The weekly rate of a shared additional pension shall be the appropriate weekly amount, unless the pensioner's entitlement to the state scheme pension credit arose before the final relevant year, in which case it shall be that amount multiplied by the relevant revaluation percentage.

(4) The appropriate weekly amount for the purposes of subsection (3) above is the weekly rate, expressed in terms of the valuation day, at which the cash equivalent, on that day, of the pensioner's entitlement, or prospective entitlement, to the shared additional pension is equal to the state scheme pension credit.

(5) The relevant revaluation percentage for the purposes of that subsection is the percentage specified, in relation to earnings factors for the tax year in which the entitlement to the state scheme pension credit arose, by the last order under section 148 of the Administration Act to come into force before the end of the final relevant year.

(6) Cash equivalents for the purposes of this section shall be calculated in accordance with regulations.

(7) In this section –

"final relevant year" means the tax year immediately preceding that in which the pensioner attains pensionable age;

"state scheme pension credit" means a credit under section 49(1)(b) of the Welfare Reform and Pensions Act 1999 (credit for the purposes of this Part of this Act);

"valuation day" means the day on which the pensioner becomes entitled to the state scheme pension credit.

55B. Reduction of shared additional pension: pension sharing

(1) The weekly rate of a shared additional pension shall be reduced as follows in any case where –

(a) the pensioner has become subject to a state scheme pension debit, and

(b) the debit is to any extent referable to the pension.

(2) If the pensioner became subject to the debit in or after the final relevant year, the weekly rate of the pension shall be reduced by the appropriate weekly amount.

(3) If the pensioner became subject to the debit before the final relevant year, the weekly rate of the additional pension shall be reduced by the appropriate weekly amount multiplied by the relevant revaluation percentage.

(4) The appropriate weekly amount for the purposes of subsections (2) and (3) above is the weekly rate, expressed in terms of the valuation day, at which the cash equivalent, on that day, of the pension mentioned in subsection (5) below is equal to so much of the debit as is referable to the shared additional pension .

(5) The pension referred to above is a notional pension for the pensioner by virtue of section 55A above which becomes payable on the later of –

(a) his attaining pensionable age, and

(b) the valuation day.

(6) For the purposes of subsection (3) above, the relevant revaluation percentage is the percentage specified, in relation to earning factors for the tax year in which the pensioner became subject to the debit, by the last order under section 148 of the Administration Act to come into force before the end of the final relevant year.

(7) Cash equivalents for the purposes of this section shall be calculated in accordance with regulations.

(8) In this section –

"final relevant year" means the tax year immediately preceding that in which the pensioner attains pensionable age;

"state scheme pension debit", means a debit under section 49(1)(a) of the Welfare Reform and Pensions Act 1999 (debit for the purposes of this Part of this Act);

"valuation day" means the day on which the pensioner became subject to the state scheme pension debit.

55C. Increase of shared additional pension where entitlement is deferred

(1) For the purposes of this section, a person's entitlement to a shared additional pension is deferred –

(a) where he would be entitled to a Category A or Category B retirement pension but for the fact that his entitlement to such a pension is deferred, if and so long as his entitlement to such a pension is deferred, and

(b) otherwise, if and so long as he does not become entitled to the shared additional pension by reason only of not satisfying the conditions of section 1 of the Administration Act (entitlement to benefit dependent on claim),

and, in relation to a shared additional pension, "period of deferment" shall be construed accordingly.

(2) Where a person's entitlement to a shared additional pension is deferred, the rate of his shared additional pension shall be increased by an amount equal to the aggregate of the increments to which he is entitled under subsection (3) below, but only if that amount is enough to increase the rate of the pension by at least 1 per cent.

(3) A person is entitled to an increment under this subsection for each complete incremental period in his period of enhancement.

(4)   The amount of the increment for an incremental period shall be 1/7th per cent. Of the weekly rate of the shared additional pension to which the person would have been entitled for the period if his entitlement had not been deferred.

(5)   Amounts under subsection (4) above shall be rounded to the nearest penny, taking any 1/2p as nearest to the next whole penny.

(6)   Where an amount under subsection (4) above would, apart from this subsection, be a sum less than 1/2p, the amount shall be taken to be zero, notwithstanding any other provision of this Act, the Pensions Act 1995 or the Administration Act.

(7)   Where one or more orders have come into force under section 150 of the Administration Act during the period of enhancement, the rate for any incremental period shall be determined as if the order or orders had come into force before the beginning of the period of enhancement.

(8)   The sums which are the increases in the rates of shared additional pensions under this section are subject to alteration by order made by the Secretary of State under section 150 of the Administration Act.

(9)   In this section –

"incremental period" means any period of six days which are treated by regulations as days of increment for the purposes of this section in relation to the person and pension in question; and

"period of enhancement", in relation to that person and that pension, means the period which –

(a)   begins on the same day as the period of deferment in question, and

(b)   ends on the same day as that period or, if earlier, on the day before the 5th anniversary of the beginning of that period.'

Undertaking not to frustrate a Pension Sharing Order

Undertaking by party with pension rights not to draw benefits under a pension scheme in such a way as to frustrate a Pension Sharing Order

AND UPON the [*petitioner*] [*respondent*] undertaking to the court and agreeing not to draw any benefits arising from his/her membership of [*name of pension scheme/personal pension policy/retirement annuity contract*] [No. . . .] with [*company*] in such form as to frustrate the provisions of paragraph [. . .] of this order

Glossary of terms

Accrual Rate   The rate at which pension benefit increases as pensionable service is completed in a final salary scheme, e.g. 1/60th for each year of pensionable service.

Accrued Benefits   The benefits in respect of service up to a specific date calculated in relation to current earnings or projected final earnings.

Added Years   The provision of additional pension by reference to additional periods of pensionable service in a final salary scheme. Added years may be provided either by transfer payments or additional voluntary contributions or augmentation.

Additional Voluntary Contributions (AVCs)   Contributions a member elects to pay over and above his normal contributions (if any) in order to secure extra benefits. The total employee contributions may not exceed 15% of earnings in any one year.

Commutation   The exchange of pension benefits at retirement for an immediate tax-free lump sum payment.

COMP   Contracted Out Money Purchase scheme.

Continuation Option   An option to effect a life assurance policy to replace the life cover provided by the pension scheme upon leaving without having to provide evidence of health.

Contracting Out   An arrangement whereby a member of a pension scheme that meets certain conditions can pay reduced National Insurance contributions and/or rebates are paid to the pension scheme, in return for which the scheme provides benefits as an alternative to SERPS/S2P.

Death in Service Benefits   Benefits provided on death before retirement, normally a lump sum and/or return of contributions, plus a widow's/dependants' pension.

Defined Contributions   A money purchase scheme where the rate of contributions is set out in the rules.

Earnings Cap   The maximum amount of earnings that may be pensioned. It applies to all schemes established after 14 March 1989 and members joining existing schemes after 31 May 1989. The current earnings limit is £102,000 for the tax year 2004/05.

Executive Pension Plan   A scheme for selected directors or employees.

Exempt Approved Scheme   An approved occupational scheme established under an irrevocable trust enjoying taxation privileges.

Expression of Wish   A means by which a member can indicate a preference as to who should receive any lump sum death benefit. The trustees of the scheme are not bound by this nomination.

Final Salary Scheme   A pension scheme where the benefit is calculated by reference to the member's pensionable earnings at or near retirement or leaving service. For example, the benefits may be 1/60th of earnings for each year of pensionable service.

Free-standing AVCs   A member of an occupational pension scheme may make additional voluntary contributions to another totally separate scheme.

Guaranteed Minimum Pension   The minimum pension which a scheme contracted out on a final salary basis before 1997 provided as one of the conditions of contracting-out.

Insured Scheme   A pension scheme where the only long term investment is an insurance policy (other than a managed fund policy).

Limited Price Indexation   Guaranteed Pension increases in line with the RPI, subject to a maximum of 5% per annum.

Lower Earnings Limit   The minimum amount which must be earned before National Insurance contributions become payable in respect of employees. Once this limit is exceeded, contributions are payable in respect of earnings both below and above this limit.

Money Purchase Scheme.   A scheme where benefits are directly determined by the value of the accumulated fund resulting from the contributions paid.

Nomination   Another term for expression of wish.

OPB   Occupational Pensions Board which was dissolved with effect from 6 April 1997.

OPRA   The Occupational Pensions Regulatory Authority which is the regulatory body overseeing compliance with the requirements of the Pensions Act 1995.

Occupational Pension   A scheme established by an employer to provide Scheme pension benefits for employees. A contribution must be made by the employer.

Pensionable Earnings   The earning upon which benefits and/or contributions are based. These could differ from actual remuneration in that they might exclude items such as bonuses, overtime and commissions but could, for example, include items such as company car allowance.

Pensionable Service   Period of qualifying employment as defined by the pension scheme rules.

Personal Pension Scheme   A money purchase scheme which may be provided by an insurance company, building society, bank or unit trust group and to which an employer is not required to contribute. These schemes came into force on 1 July 1988 replacing the previous self-employed retirement annuity and may be taken out by both the employed and self-employed.

Preserved Benefits   Benefits arising on an individual ceasing to be an active member of a pension scheme and payable at a later date.

Protected Rights   The benefits under a contracted-out personal pension scheme or a COMP deriving from the minimum contributions necessary for contracting-out.

Retained Benefits   Retirement or death benefits in respect of an employee's earlier service with a former employer or earlier period of self employment which have benefited from tax privileges.

Retirement Annuity Contract (RAC)   The predecessors of personal pensions (often called section 226 policies). No new retirement annuities could be sold after 30 June 1988 but existing contracts can be continued. The fund available to purchase pension at retirement is dependent upon contributions paid and investment performance.

S2P   The State Second Pension which replaced SERPS from 6 April 2002 onwards.

Safeguarded Rights   That part of a shared pension which is directly attributable to the pension scheme member's Contracted-Out benefits.

Salary Sacrifice   An agreement between employer and employee whereby the employee gives up part of his salary and the employer makes a corresponding increase in the level of pension contributions.

Self-administered   A scheme whereby the assets are invested by the trustees or external investment manager.

SERPS   The State Earnings Related Pension Scheme which is paid in addition to the basic flat rate pension in respect of earnings up to 5 April 2002.

Stakeholder Scheme   A Money Purchase Scheme established to comply with various requirements introduced pursuant to the Welfare Reform and Pensions Act 1999 and aimed at individuals with an income between approximately £9,000 and £18,000.

State Pensionable Age   The age from which pensions are normally payable by the State Scheme, currently 65 for men and 60 for women. To become 65 for both men and women by the year 2020; with a sliding scale for women between the years 2010 and 2020.

Statutory Scheme   A retirement benefit scheme established by statute usually for the benefit of public sector employees.

Transfer Payment   A payment made by the trustees of one pension scheme to the trustees of another enabling the receiving pension scheme to provide alternative benefits.

Unapproved Scheme   Benefits can exceed those of approved schemes. Revenue approval need not be sought but the usual tax concessions are not available.

Unit Linked Pension   The scheme funds are notionally invested in units of an investment fund and the value of the fund varies according to the value of the units.

Upper Earnings Limit   The maximum amount of earnings on which National Insurance contributions are payable.

Vested Rights   The benefits under the scheme to which a member is unconditionally entitled were he to leave service including related benefits for dependants.

Index

Solicitors and Money Laundering

A Compliance Handbook

Peter Camp

This authoritative handbook clearly
demonstrates how the new anti-
money laundering laws apply to
solicitor's practices. It highlights
areas of practice most at risk and
gives practical advice on how to
introduce anti-money laundering procedures enabling firms
to recognise and report suspicious transactions.

The practical nature of the book is enhanced by helpful
precedents, guidance material and statutory material, including:

- a precedent money laundering manual
- client identification form, internal reporting form and NCIS
  reporting forms
- official NCIS guidance on reporting suspicious transactions.

Written by a recognised expert, taking account of the latest Law
Society guidelines it is essential reading for solicitors and their
professional advisers looking to meet compliance objectives.

Available from Marston Book Services:
Tel. 01235 465 656.

1 85328 920 5
288 pages
£49.95
Sept. 2004

The Law Society